THE BLUE RI~~L~~

AUTUMN LEAVES
AND
PUMPKINS PLEASE

STEPHANIE NICHOLE

Copyright

Autumn Leaves and Pumpkins Please is a work of fiction. All names, characters, locations, and incidents are the products of the author's imagination or are used fictiously. Any resemblance to actual events, locales, or persons, living or dead, is entirely coincidental.

Editing by KP Editing
Cover Design by KP Designs
- www.kpdesignshop.com
Published by Kingston Publishing Company
- www.kingstonpublishing.com

Table of Contents

Dedication

To all of those who have faced fire in whatever form that may be and have risen from the ashes.

Playlist

In the Clear by Foo Fighters

The Good Ones by Gabby Barrett

Messy by Chase Rice

Whiskey and Rain by Michael Ray

Pretty Heart by Parker McCollum

Pretty Damn Close by Gary Allan

Truth About You by Mitchell Tenpenny

Try Missing You by Jon Langston

Love Ain't by Eli Young Band

Guinevere by Eli Young Band

Crazy Girl by Eli Young Band

Home by Foo Fighters

PROLOGUE

Capri
16 years old

I sit on the deflating air mattress in my roach infested room. The white ceiling above me is rotting. Spots of discoloration show through from where the roof has leaked. Outside my bedroom door, I can hear my drunk, and probably high, father as he beats and yells at my stepmother. A part of me still feels like I should go and try to help her, but she is literally the epitome of the evil stepmother. She despises me, and she's never come to help me even in the darkest of times. His angry, slurred voice bellows through the paper-thin walls of the trailer.

Stray tears slip down my cheeks and I swipe them away angrily. My father has always been a world class piece of shit. He's more concerned about his brothers in the motorcycle club he runs with. Their main concern is the drugs and women they sell. Nothing else matters. It doesn't matter that I'm only sixteen, trying to make it through high school and actually do something with my life. It doesn't matter that when he's drunk off his ass or high out of his mind, that I have to barricade my bedroom door to keep his 'brothers' from coming in. Nothing matters to him.

My mother couldn't handle it anymore, not that I totally blamed her, so she bolted. She left me in the rundown trailer my father calls home, in the worst neighborhood, alone. She now has a perfect husband with a new perfect family. The internet has allowed me to keep up with her throughout the years. Although, I'm not sure why I do. It's just a vivid reminder that I've never been good enough for anyone to choose. I've been forgotten by her and beaten by him, but tonight I get out.

Billy isn't my forever, but he is my way out. I'll climb on the back of his motorcycle, but we won't get a happily ever after. He's my escape from being trailer park trash just like my father. My worn backpack is packed with everything I own, which isn't much. I'm ready and I'm waiting. A tap on the window causes me to jerk my head up. The trailer has gone silent, so I guess my dad is done with his angry outburst. He's either passed out or snorting crap up his nose again.

Billy's blonde head of hair appears in my window with his eyes as dark as the night sky. He's three years older than me and hangs with another motorcycle club a couple of towns over. A few months ago, my best friend, Rachel, took her parents car and we snuck into a little dive bar to watch a band play live. Billy was there banging on the drums. It wasn't love at first sight but there was a flicker of something that caught my attention. I open the window. "Are you ready, babe?" he asks. I nod my head and pass him my backpack. He slips it on his shoulders and then reaches for me. He helps me out the window and we run back to his bike parked outside of the trailer park. I don't even bother to look back. What's the point? There's nothing to miss there and nothing will miss me.

****

20 years old

I scan the room, double checking to make sure I didn't miss anything important. Eddie is passed out in our bed, so I know I need to move quickly. There's always the possibility of him waking up sooner, and if he does, there will be hell to pay. I cringe at the thought. As quietly as possible, I rush through the house. What little I own I shoved into a Wal-Mart sack. My purse hangs from my shoulder. I grab the keys to the car and rush out the door.

Eddie wasn't supposed to be my forever but I didn't think it'd turn out like this. You know when they say you'll marry someone like your father…. I may not have married Eddie, but he is exactly like my father. There was something about him. He walked on the wild side, a brush with danger that excited me. That should have been my first sign to avoid him, but instead I rushed into things with him, and look where it got me.

When I get into the car, I catch a glimpse of myself in the rearview mirror. The bruise was lighter, but now it's darkening again and swollen. It's impossible to stay out of his way when he needs a fix, and his anger is flaring. I back out of the driveway and fly down the dirt road to the highway. I don't look back because there's nothing there anyways. My plan is to drive until the gas runs out, take what cash I have and buy a bus ticket as far away from here as possible. I'm always running. I've been running away from my series of bad decisions since I was sixteen. All I wanted to do was escape the hell I called home. In the long run, I just made my life a bigger mess. Always chasing things that don't exist. One of these days, I'll realize I'm fine on my own.

****

24 years old

I lie on the cold tile floor of the clean kitchen. The kitchen that was pristinely white is now smeared with blood. My blood. The ache in my ribs only causes my head to pound harder. My left eye is swollen shut and blood leaks from the cut on my lip. I don't know how long I've laid here, my heart shattering. He was supposed to be my happily ever after, but instead he became the biggest monster of all. The devil in disguise.

He said all the perfect things and it felt so sincere. It felt real and I fell for it. For so long, I just wanted someone to choose me, and he did. I just didn't realize what he was choosing me for. The big, beautiful house he put me in became my prison. His words left me sliced open and his body became a weapon of mass destruction. One wrong move and I paid over and over again. No apology was ever good enough because in his eyes I was never good enough. The only thing he truly wanted was a punching bag to suffice the chip on his shoulder.

I thought I was done running, but I was wrong. The plan forms in my head. He'll be at work tomorrow. I'll pack what I can and run once again. I won't look back because there's nothing left here for me. I'm beginning to think I was better off as trailer trash. This house was no safer. The man I 'loved' was no better than the father I ran from.

Pushing myself up, wincing at the ache, I find a determination in myself that I've never felt before. I'm not running. I'm leaving and I don't need anyone. It's me, myself and I from now on. No more looking for happily ever after. It doesn't exist anyways. I'm going to leave this hell that I walked into in the form of pretty, expensive things and I'm never looking back. This is the last time I let my heart make a decision for me. From now on, I go with my brain, and I only consider myself. No one will ever lay another hand on me again. I refuse to be another statistic.

ONE

Capri

The sun beams through the slats of the vertical blinds from the living room. It's my day off from Bee's Batter, but it still seems weird to not already be at work. I miss the bakery when I'm not there. That place feels like it gives me a purpose and that's something I've never had. My loft apartment is unusually chilly. When I sit up, I instantly reach for my oversized, teal sweatshirt that is thrown on the large round chair sitting in the corner of the room. I slip it on and throw my bird nest of bedhead into a messy bun. My loft apartment isn't much, but it's all mine and affordable, which is all that matters to me. As I get out of bed, I realize I left the windows in the living room below me cracked open. That explains the chilliness of the apartment, at least.

I pad down the stairs to the living space below. Last night, I painted on the blank canvas until my eyes bled all the colors together. I knew it was time to call it a night then. Closing the windows must have slipped my mind. As I make my way over to them, I stop to pet, Thora, my Tabby cat. Really, she's hardly mine. I found her in the alley that leads to my apartment right after I moved to Blue Ridge. She seemed just as lost as I did at the time. It took a few days and about ten cans of tuna to get her to trust me enough to let me pet her and another week before I was able to catch her and visit the vet. Thora received a clean bill of health and moved in with me. We've been roommates ever since. She purrs as I pet her orange, fluffy coat. "Good morning, Sweet Girl."

As I make my way towards the three large windows sitting in the middle of the exposed brick wall of my living room, the canvas from last night catches my eye. I detour making my way to it. The way the colors bleed together calms something in my soul. That piece of me that is always looking for happiness but knows I can never truly find it. Blue Ridge is the first place I've felt content though, so I call it home.

Movement from across the alley that my living room faces catches my eye. When I look out, I see Jayse Lyon in his backyard, shirtless in all his glory. He's currently cutting wood for whatever job he's currently working on. From what I know about him, aside from the fact that he is breathtakingly handsome, he's the town's handyman. If something needs to be fixed in town you call Jayse. Before that he was the town's golden boy. Quarterback of the high school's football team was recruited to play for the Florida Gators but turned it down to become a firefighter. A year later, something tragic happened leaving half of his beautifully sculpted body scared with angry red rivets in his skin from the burns he sustained. Apparently, he quit his job and became a recluse and handyman.

A man is the last thing I need in my life. Every time one shows up, it only makes things messier. The last time I left one was the last time. I made myself that vow and for the past three years I've stuck with it. I'll continue to keep my vow for the next thirty years at this point. There's no point in getting off track. No matter how handsome he is with his tall, muscled body, tanned skin, shoulder length chocolate colored hair and intense gray eyes. He's broody with an arm of tattoos and drives a motorcycle when he's not working. Yep, he's everything I don't need.

As if he can feel my eyes on him, he looks up. A chunk of hair breaks loose from the low ponytail he wears it in. It falls over his eyes, clinging to his sweaty forehead. I duck away from the window. My heart beats rapidly in my chest. I'm sure he saw me but it's okay to look. I just won't touch.

After a few minutes, I pull the windows shut, making sure they're locked because you can never be too sure and then head through my living room to the kitchen. When I get to the coffee pot and open the cabinet, I realize I'm out of coffee. I should have guessed. There's no way I can start my day without coffee, so I head back upstairs to my bedroom and get dressed for the day. A little while later, I head out to my charcoal gray Chevy Sonic. As I slip behind the steering wheel of my car, Jayse comes back out into his backyard. His eyes scan over the car and I'm thankful for the tinted windows.

The engine comes to life, and I slip on my sunglasses since I actually put my contacts in today. Foo Fighters blare through the speakers and I head down the alley to Bee's Batter. Most of the rush should have cleared off by now so grabbing a coffee and something to eat should be easy. As I enter, Warbee, the owner of the bakery and my manager, looks up. Her red hair is pulled back in a ponytail. She smiles. "Girl, don't you ever take the day off?"

I laugh. "Well, I took it like you told me I had to, but I'm out of coffee at my place and you know me and my coffee."

"That I do. You can't function without it." She moves behind the counter making my caramel cinnamon latte. I look at all the baked things she has this morning, and my stomach decides it wants a maple pumpkin scone with praline pecans. Warbee slides the coffee towards me. "See anything else you'd like?"

"You know it. My mouth is basically watering at the scones." Warbee wraps me a couple of the scones up and slips them into one of the new mint-colored boxes with a black and white bow on top. "I just love these little boxes we got, but you didn't have to waste one on me."

Warbee beams. "They're awesome, right. Teaganne found them and I knew we had to have them."

Teaganne is Warbee's best friend. She's a fashion designer turned interior designer as well as event planner. Warbee and Teaganne own BeeTeag Planning which has been great for the bakery. "Y'all do make a pretty good team."

"We do, don't we?" Warbee smiles. "Now, get out of here and enjoy your day off."

I laugh. "You're one to talk. You're here every day. "

Warbee leans over the counter next to the register. "When Rocker isn't at home, the bakery feels more like home than any other place I could be."

My heart tugs. Rocker is Warbee's fiancé, really soon to be husband. They are one of those ridiculously cute couples that could make you believe in love. They've put me to the test plenty of times, but my heart is as cold as ice when it comes to the thought. One too many bad decisions with men who were even worse. Although, I do envy what Rocker and Warbee share. "That makes sense. I guess I'm going to run into Atlanta and pick out a new hair color." I'm not sure why I constantly change my hair color. I often think that it's because it's the one thing I can control in my crazy messed up world.

"I can't wait to see what you pick. You know I live vicariously through you."

I smile and head out of the bakery. I recognize the coco-colored truck that Jayse drives. It's sitting at the red light. As I climb into my Sonic, I can feel his eyes on me. My heart speeds up, but I hold my breath in a desperate attempt to calm it. I can't afford to let it start doing the thinking again.

TWO

Jayse

*S*moke coils around me, wrapping around my body like the devil's hands. Attempting to drag me to hell, but he doesn't realize I'm already there. Blistering heat is felt all around me, even my gear can't protect me from the scorching heat of the flames as they close in around me. Glass shatters from the heat, and I watch in horror as the picture frame hanging beside me on the hallway wall slips down, until it lands on the ashen floor. The faces already warped from the destruction of the fire.

Panic coils in my body and without thinking, I blindly charge into the thick smoke. I can't see anything in front of me, but I know there are two people that need to be rescued. A child and a mother and I'll do anything I can to get to them. My life doesn't matter. Just theirs. All the doors in the hallway are wide open except for one. The master bedroom is closed. I rush forward, but the door is blocked. Taking a few steps back I kick and kick until finally the wood begins to give.

I sit up straight in my bed. Sweat soaks me and the sheets I'm tangled up in. My breath comes in tight gasps. Eyes water from the panic I can still feel as if I'm still stuck in the burning house. Sweat drenched hair clings around my neck where it has escaped from the hair tie it was in. The dark locks cling to the angry ridges that mar my skin. The constant reminder of a nightmare I can't escape, a failure I will never be able to live with. Angrily, I kick the sheet I'm tangled in out of the way and climb out of the bed on wobbly legs. The house is pitch black, but I know my way around as I make my way to the kitchen. When I pull the fridge door open, I'm blasted with the ice-cold air. It cools my heated skin, drying the sweat. The fridge is stocked, but there is nothing to take away the images that are so vividly etched into my mind. I quit drinking alcohol a few years ago so I grab the gallon of water sitting inside, pull the lid off, and chug it until the taste of ash no longer lingers on my tongue.

When the fridge door shuts, I slide down until my ass hits the floor, bury my head in my hands, and try to remember the deep breathing exercises my therapist told me about. Panic still courses through my veins, eating me from the inside out. This is exactly why I left the fire station. There's no way I could ever face it again. I'd just end up becoming another person they'd have to rescue.

Now, I just go around town and fix anything and everything they need. If something breaks, they all call me. I'm fine with that. The money keeps my bills paid and food on my table. There's only one problem. Blue Ridge is small, and everyone knows every damn thing about my life. My failures sit in the forefront of their mind so when they see me the sympathy in their eyes makes me nauseous. Heads fall to the side in a tilt to remind me of everything I've lost. The blatant reminder of how far I've fallen in their eyes since my golden boy status of Blue Ridge.

Eventually, the anger raging in my bones chases the panic from my blood and I feel like I'm back on level ground again. The sun will be rising in a bit so there's no point in going back to bed. As I stand up, I stretch my achy muscles and head back to the bedroom. Yanking the sheets from the bed, I march out the back door to one of the two small house-like sheds. One is for my tools and equipment I need for my job. The other is the laundry room. Every time I relive that nightmare, I have to wash the sheets. Once they are in the washer, I head back inside. I stop to open all the blinds in the small house that I call home. It's not much, but I don't need a lot.

When I purchased the home, it was a small two bedroom. It was one of the older homes in the area, but it still had a lot of life left in it. All it really needed was someone that could fix it up. A year later, and it was exactly how I wanted. It transformed into more of an open floor plan with new hardwood floors instead of the original carpet. The wood paneling on the walls is gone now, too. Most of the work was painting everything and the kitchen. The kitchen got gutted and was completely redone as well as the bathroom.

When I reach my bedroom, I head straight for the bathroom where I start the shower. While it's warming up, I go back to the kitchen and start the coffee maker. I feel like I'm running around in circles today, but I'm usually like this when that memory rears its ugly head. From my kitchen window, I notice movement from across the alley. Capri Owens is my first thought but it's not her. It's the neighbor that shares the building she lives in. Ella Mae who owns the Spins Dance Studio. Capri's blinds are closed, but I can see them moving which means she probably left her windows cracked again. I've noticed it seems to be a habit of hers. Eventually, I head back to the bathroom to find the steam is building. For a moment, that panic ebbs its way back up my throat until I close my eyes and count to ten, reminding myself it's just steam and not smoke. Once my breathing calms, I strip down and climb under the scalding hot water.

By the time I get out of the shower, my skin is screaming in protest. Wiping the fog from the mirror, I grimace at the bags under my eyes. Sleep has not been a friend of mine lately and it's starting to show. I comb through my brown shoulder length hair before tying it back in a ponytail. After I slip on a pair of jeans and my work boots, I stop to make my coffee, black and bitter, just how I like it and head outside. The sun is up now, but the town is still quiet. I grab the wood for my next project and start measuring the pieces.

Halfway through, I notice movement from Capri's apartment. When I look up, she ducks away from the window. She is one hell of a mystery. She is also the last thing I need but I can't help but look every time I see her. The girl is so damn gorgeous, and she doesn't even know it, but something about how skittish she is, tells me she hasn't had the easiest life. Her seafoam green eyes are enough to knock the air right out of your lungs. She's unique with her ever changing hair color, huge false eyelashes, nose ring that often matches whatever color of oversized glasses she's wearing that day, and a wardrobe that consists mostly of skinny jeans, band and horror t-shirts, and Vans or Converse. I know she's creative because I've watched from the shadows of my porch as she stands in front of her window and moves a brush over a canvas. The canvas sits off to the side, so I can never see what she creates, but something tells me it's stunning just like her profile while she creates the painting. Capri is quiet and closed off except for when she's around Warbee and her group of friends. A few weeks ago, I did a revamp on Bee's Batter, Warbee's bakery, and that was the most I had seen of Capri since living here. Around all of them she laughed, joked, and had a great time. Her voice is sweet like maple syrup.

I don't see Capri again until I'm coming back out of the house and she's slipping into her car. All I catch is a glimpse of her fading purple hair, before she disappears behind the dark tint of the windows. Even though I can't see her, it doesn't stop me from trying to. She peels down the alley and I watch as she goes. Why do I want to know her story so damn much?

THREE

Capri

These Days by Foo Fighters blare through the speakers of my car as I sing loudly and off key to the lyrics. There's always been something about the lyrics in the Foo Fighters songs that really hit me. My car is loaded down. I managed to squeeze four blank canvases into my tiny backseat. Everything else is crammed into my small trunk. I used to order the canvases online because they were cheaper, but a lot of the time they would come in damaged or get damaged from the weather when they were delivered to my apartment while I was at work. Plus, knowing that I get to help a small, home owned business makes me feel better about the money I'm spending.

As I pulled back into Blue Ridge I decided to stop by Bee's Batter. I could really use a decaf sleepy time tea. I feel incredibly wired from my excitement with the art supplies I bought today. Instead of fighting to go to sleep, I could just swing by and grab something to help me unwind. I'm shocked to see the bakery is still pretty packed for it to be almost closing time. Once I find a parking place across the street, I stand by and wait for a chance to dart across. The older, blue Ford truck that Jayse uses for his handyman business comes into view. My foolish heart stutters in my chest. As he approaches, I notice his eyes squinting in my direction. He studies me and I hold my breath. When he gets closer, he comes to a full stop. Talk about a deer in the headlights. I stand there, completely frozen. Eventually, Jayse notices the headlights approaching behind him and motions for me to cross the street. Something inside me clicks and I jog as fast as I can while trying not to look silly.

When I reach the door of the bakery, I look back over my shoulder, trying to be discreet, but to my disappointment Jayse is already gone. The bell above the door rings throughout the bakery. Warbee looks up from where she's wiping the counter. "Capri, it's your day off and you still show up here." Warbee, the owner of Bee's Batter and my boss, laughs from behind the counter. She's a fiery redhead with hazel eyes and fair skin. She normally has large, oversized glasses and dresses pretty simple.

"You're one to talk," I tease her back. We have the same conversation every time we see each other in the bakery on a day off. Just this we had this same conversation.

Warbee shrugs her slim shoulders. "I own the place. What's your excuse?"

"Sometimes, this bakery feels more like home than my actual home," I admit. It may sound sad but it's true. Warbee took me in when I first stumbled into town. When I walked into the bakery, I barely had anything left, but she stuffed me full of sweets until I thought I would burst. Afterwards, she asked me about my plans, which I had none. To be honest, I hadn't thought that far ahead. She insisted I stay with her until I figured it out. I can still remember fighting back the tears that pricked at the back of my eyes. I couldn't imagine anyone being so kind. Warbee wasn't nosey, just incredibly kind. The next morning, she offered me a temporary job for as long as I needed it. She never asked for my story, and I was relieved. Of course, now she knows everything, but she also knows my job isn't temporary. After a couple of weeks in Blue Ridge, I knew I had found a place to call home. It was kind and safe.

She gives me an understanding smile. "I get that." Silence falls between us for a few minutes, before she shakes her head. "So, what can I do for you?"

I sigh and yawn a bit. "I wanted to get a decaf sleepy time tea."

Warbee laughs. "Are you sure? You just yawned; you know?"

"Yes," I tell her, with a laugh. "I know the moment I get home and lay down I won't be tired at all."

"Okay!" Warbee gets the tea steeping before she comes around the counter. "So, tomorrow I want you to take the day off again."

"What?" I always work six days a week. It was my request. The bakery is always a little shorthanded and I love to work. It keeps me busy and out of trouble. The last thing I need is extra down time.

"Look, I know you like to work six days a week, but this week you're getting two days off in a row. You've earned it. Sleep in and relax for a while." Warbee heads back around the counter and pours the tea in a hot cup to go. "Now, go get some sleep.

I take the tea after trying to pay Warbee. Try being the key word, because she just walked away telling me my money was no good. I end up dropping the five-dollar bill into the tip jar and head back to my car so I can get home. The alley is dark except for the few porch lights from the houses and buildings. As I climb out of the car, I feel as if someone is watching me. It's silly really because I know that's not possible. After collecting my tea, purse, and some of the sacks from my trunk, I head inside. The bottom floor of the building is the laundry room, office space for the owner, and mailboxes. The staircase to the right leads upstairs to the two apartments that Ella Mae and I rent. However, I only take one step inside when the slosh of water can be heard as my shoes soak with water. "What in the world?" I feel around for the light switch and to my surprise the bottom floor is standing in water. The hideous aqua tile glistens under the water and for a moment it's actually kind of pretty. Gurgling noises come from the laundry room directly ahead of me. I wade through the water carefully and sure enough, one of the washers is spurting water into the floor. Carefully, I make my way back outside. Tossing my bags back into the trunk I fish out my cell phone. Clark, the owner of the building, is out of town. He's a forty something year old single man who goes to Florida to visit his parents every October and December for the holidays. We don't have a maintenance man. Usually, when things break, Clark calls in Jayse. I dial Clark and wait for him to answer.

Laughter fills the phone before I ever hear his raspy voice. "Capri?"

"Yes, it's me. I'm so sorry to bother you, Clark. I just got home, and the entire bottom floor of the building is standing in water. It seems to be coming from a washer."

"Oh goodness. Can you tell if Jayse is home?" he asks.

I turn around and study the small but cute house. There is a faint light, I'm assuming coming from a television, that I can see. "I think he might be."

"Great. If you can go grab him and tell him to email me a bill." Clark sighs heavily. "I'm really sorry to put this off on you."

"It's not a problem. I'll run over and if for some reason he isn't home I'll call you back," I tell him. The last thing I want to do is bother Clark on his little vacation. I certainly didn't mean to make him feel bad, but his voice sounded that way.

"Thank you. If he's not home, I have his cell phone number and I can call him so just call me back."

I nod my head as I head across the alley. "I will." We disconnect the call without bothering to say goodbye. Hesitation hits me as I reach for the back gate of Jayse's fence. It almost feels like I'm invading his privacy, but Clark did tell me to do this. Shaking my head, I flip the hinge and march through his dark yard and up his back porch. My hand fists and I knock on the door, harder than I intended, as knots form in my stomach.

When the door opens, the version of Jayse in front of me is the last one expected. His hair is loose and skimming the skin on his shoulders. Shirtless so that every angry scar is visible, as well as all of his well-defined muscles and tattoos. Red basketball shorts hang low on his hips, the band of his underwear just peeping above. His eyes narrow. "Capri?"

I fidget for a moment, the knots in my stomach intensifying. "I'm sorry to bug you, but there's a water leak so I called Clark and he asked me to come and get you."

"Where's the water leak?" he asks.

"The whole bottom floor is standing in water right now. One of the washers, I think."

Instantly, Jayse starts to gather his hair back and I watch in fascination as he ties it back with a hair tie on his wrist. "Let me get dressed and grab my tools and I'll head that way." I nod my head and turn around, briskly walking back to my car. I'm standing by the front door of the building when Jayse appears in front of me. "So, I'm going to clean up the mess and cut the machine off. More than likely, it will need some parts that I don't keep on hand, but I'm sure I can get it fixed first thing tomorrow."

"I'm sure that works. Clark is out of town."

Jayse nods his head. "Visiting his parents, right?"

"Yeah. What's this machine?"

"A Shop Vac, is what I call it. Basically, it will suck up the water," he explains.

I won't admit it in front of him, but I didn't know those types of machines existed. I was just dreading the amount of mopping it was going to take. Jayse heads inside and I follow closely behind him. A low whistle comes from him as he assesses the bottom floor. "It's bad, right?"

He glances over his shoulder. "It's not great." I start to step around him to show him which machine I saw throwing the water everywhere, but I slip and the next thing I know I'm falling. I land with a splash, my head bouncing down into the water, slapping against the tile of the floor. Strong arms wrap around my waist and pull me towards the staircase. I'm a little dizzy and can't fully focus on anything right now. However, it doesn't slip my attention just how good his arms feel.

FOUR

Jayse

The dull thud hits my ears, muffled from the water currently standing on the floor, but I know before I even turn around what it is. Capri is lying in the water, her head staining the clear aqua a bright red. Instantly, all the training that used to be part of my day-to-day life kicks in and I rush forward pulling her from the water and carrying her to the stairs. I cradled her against my chest, her soaked clothes seeping through mine, cooling my heated skin. Her head has a pretty nasty cut, but it doesn't need stitches. "Capri, can you tell me how many fingers I'm holding up?" I ask her. We go through a series of questions, all of which she manages to answer correctly.

"I'm okay. My head just hurts. Does it need stitches?" There's a worried look in her eyes.

I shake my head. "No, in my professional opinion it should heal just fine. We just need to get it cleaned up and bandaged."

"Professional opinion? No offense, but I'm not sure I should take my handyman's opinion on head injuries as professional," she tells me with a giggle. I watch in awe as her entire face lights up with a small smile.

"Well, I'm not just any handyman. Once upon a time, I was a firefighter. I've had lots of training. So no don't trust the handyman's opinion, but trust the firefighters." Her eyes widen and the worry morphs into something serious. Her slender hand tentatively reaches out, brushing against the jagged scars that mar a good portion of my body.

Her head tilts to the side as she studies them under the muted light the building offers. Capri's fingertips feel like ice against my skin. The scars always feel hot to me, but I think it's the memories that are attached to them that actually trick my mind into believing that. The black color of nail polish glistens when the lights hit it as she continues to trace the rigid outlines. Emotion or something else like it clogs my throat and I have to swallow everything back down. I'm not sure when was the last time I spoke of my previous life. I've spent so much energy distancing myself from it. Constantly, reminding myself that I'm not who I once was. When Capri speaks, her voice is barely a whisper, "Is that how you got these?" Her seafoam green eyes meet mine, the simple sincerity swimming in them.

I nod my head. "Yeah," my own voice the volume of a whisper. Almost as if we'll shatter this fragile moment if we speak any louder. "I need to shut the washer's water off and go grab my first aid kit."

"I have a first aid kit upstairs."

My fingers gently sweep a damp, stray strand away from the cut. "Okay, let me get the water turned off and then we'll get this cleaned up." She winces slightly as my fingertips brush against it. I sit her down on the stairs and carefully, rush down to the laundry room and turn the water off to the machine. When I reach the stairs again Capri is standing. "Are you ready?"

She blushes. "I'm okay. I can take care of it. There's no need for you to fuss over me. This is nothing compared to what I've had before." Her eyes dart away from mine, and there's something about it that makes me wonder what she means by that comment.

I climb the stairs. "It's not a fuss. I'm not going to leave you to take care of it on your own. Besides, you could have a concussion, so I don't feel right leaving you alone right now."

"Jayse, I'm fine, really."

She starts to climb the stairs and I step in front of her, blocking her path. "I'm sure you are, but I'm still not leaving you." We stare at each other for a few moments, until finally she rolls her eyes and says, "fine." Once she agrees, I step aside and follow her up to her apartment. "Shoot," she mumbles, as she feels around in her pockets.

"What's wrong?"

Capri sighs heavily. "I must have left my keys out by my car when I went back out."

"I'll go grab them." I headed back outside to Capri's car. It's a good thing we're in Blue Ridge where very little crime occurs because her purse, keys, and sacks are all lying on the trunk of her car. I gather the items and head back inside. When I reach Capri, I hand her the keys and her purse.

Her seafoam green eyes scan my hands. "You didn't have to grab all that."

My shoulders shrug and she watches the movement intently. "I didn't mind."

Capri turns back to the door and unlocks it. When she pushes it open, the smell of pumpkin and spice cascades out into the hallway between the two doors. This building is a three-story industry warehouse that Clark bought years ago after it was vacated. He had the top two floors renovated to create the two loft apartments where Capri and Ella Mae live. Capri flips the light switch and the area floods with light from the overhead fixtures. We're standing in a small entryway where a closet just sits beside the door. Capri hangs her purse there and moves through the place. I can see the all-white kitchen from here and the living room it opens up to. The living room is bright. A bright red couch sits across from the TV. Blue, purple, and lime green pillows are scattered across it of every shape and size. A stark white chair sits to the side of it with a vibrant purple blanket lying across the back of it. Tall, silver floor lamps sit at either end of the couch and all the furniture is whitewashed wood. It stands out against the wood floors. Directly in front of us are the windows that line the back of the building, the ones I often watch Capri though. In the corner is a large easel with a half-painted canvas sitting on it. A sheet, stained with every color known to man sits under it. "The first aid kit is upstairs in the bathroom."

I follow behind Capri as we head upstairs. Her bedroom is just as bright. Neon purple bedding and rugs cover the area. The same whitewashed wood furniture up here as well. I notice the book sitting on the nightstand. War and Peace, definitely not what I expected Capri to read. She opens one of the two doors to her right. The bathroom is rather dull compared to the rest of the place. A couple of soft pink towels hang as well as a soft pink shower curtain. Capri bends down and opens the cabinet under the sink.

When she turns around, she hands me the first aid kit. I look around before motioning for her to sit on the toilet seat. Carefully, I work on cleaning up the cut, doctoring it and placing a bandage on it. Neither of us say anything as I work. The silence isn't uncomfortable, but it's heated. Capri is like a siren to me. She calls to me without meaning to, without saying a word. She always has, ever since she moved to Blue Ridge. Of course, it was my luck that she ended up living directly across the alley from me. So close, but never able to touch. I finish up and take a step back. "All done."

She lightly feels around her head. "Thanks." We pick up the bathroom then head back downstairs. I stop when the three large canvases catch my eye. All stark white with paints of black, gray and bright colors of red. The first is a pair of hands clenching a bright red heart, the hands and heart wrapped in barbed wire, blood dripping from where it cuts into the flesh. The second is a set of colorless eyes, one shaded giving the image of a bruise, tears slip from the bottom lashes, bright red as if she is crying blood. The last one is a pair of lips, the barbed wire is woven in and out of them, blood dripping from them as well. I have a sinking feeling I know the answer to the question I'm about to ask. "Who painted these?"

Capri looks away as a blush color her cheeks. "I did."

"Wow, they're amazing."

She shakes her head. "No, I was just goofing around."

My hands stuff into the pockets of my jeans. "I won't pretend to know anything about art but these... I can feel the pain coming off them, so they have to be good." Capri smiles, but it's small and sad and I hate to think of how she captured such a raw emotion like pain into three simple paintings. "So, I should get downstairs and get the water cleaned up. I'm pretty sure you have a mild concussion so you should--"

Capri cuts me off. "Not my first concussion, so I know the routine. No need to worry about me Jayse but thank you again for doctoring the cut. I really do appreciate it."

Her confession tears at a part of my soul. Capri always seems a little standoffish. Originally, when she first arrived, she seemed skittish. She watched her surroundings like a hawk, her guard never went down. I can't even imagine what she's been through. I nod my head. "Okay, if you need anything just give me a call or come over." Capri nods her head and I turn around to leave. Some part of me, which is odd, wants to stay right here with her.

FIVE

Capri

I awake to knocking coming from my front door. When I roll over and check the time on the clock, I jump out of bed in a hurry. I'm late for work. Grabbing my cell phone from the nightstand I quickly hold the speed dial number for Warbee, as I rush down the stairs to answer the front door. Warbee picks up on the second ring. "Hey, how are you feeling?" Her voice is calm and steady.

"I'm so, so sorry. I must have forgotten to set my alarm last night when I went to bed. I'll be there in a few minutes," I explain, breathless.

Warbee laughs. "It's okay. Jayse told me what happened. Jolie came in today so it's all good."

"Jayse told you?" I ask. Another knock comes from the door.

"Yeah, he was waiting for me when I pulled up to the bakery."

My eyebrows pull together in confusion. I tiptoe to see out of the peep hole and there he is…. Jayse. "Okay, well I'll make it up to Jolie. Thank you for understanding. I need to go because someone is at the door, but I'll be there tomorrow." I yank the door open and Jayse is leaning against the door frame, mint green paper bag and drink holder from the bakery in his hands. His gray eyes meet mine. "This is a first."

He chuckles and it makes my stomach coil in anticipation. It's seriously one of the best sounds in the world. "Good morning to you, too. You're not a morning person, are you?"

"What tipped you off?" I bite back.

"Well, I did come bearing goodies so maybe the little monster would like to go hide and return Capri to us?"

I can't fight the laugh that bubbles out of me. "Depends on the goodies."

He holds up his hand with the items from the bakery. "Decaf coffee and tea for you as well as one of Warbee's latest creations. Something to do with apple butter. It's a pastry of some sort. I can't remember what she called it exactly."

Stepping away from the door, I motion for him to enter. "You may pass."

"Well thank you, my lady." I led us over to my small, two-seat dining room table.

Jayse passes me two of the three drink cups before digging into the bag and sliding the pastry across to me. "First of all, why are my drinks decaf? Coffee is life."

"Agreed, but caffeine is bad for a concussion, so you get decaf."

I roll my eyes. "I feel fine."

He plants his elbows on the table and his chin in his hands. His eyes hold me motionless. "You may feel fine, but you took a nasty hit to that pretty head of yours so don't push it."

"So, is this firefighter Jayse or handyman Jayse talking?"

A sad look courses through his eyes for a moment. "Both." His entire demeanor has crumbled. Moments ago, he was flirty, and he almost seemed carefree. Now, it seems he's back to his broody normal self I've known him as.

Pulling the tissue paper back from the pastry, I smile. "It's a croissant filled with apple butter." He looks back up at me, a questioning look on his face. I point to the croissant sitting on the table.

He smiles. "So, that's what it's called." I watch as his large hands pick up the croissant and take a large bite. Jayse chews for a moment as I watch his jaw work before giving me a thumbs up.

"I really do appreciate all of this, but you didn't have to do it. I mean, going to tell Warbee what happened and bringing me breakfast." Thora appears around the kitchen. She darts forward, apparently excited about the company. Jayse scoops her up and cuddles her. Her purrs are heard from across the table.

"Who is this pretty girl?"

I smile. "The love of my life. That's Thora."

Jayse continues to cuddle Thora until he places her in his lap. She seems incredibly content. "Also, I know I didn't have to do any of that, but I wanted to. You don't seem like the type that will take it easy, so I figured I'd better let Warbee know beforehand."

"I guess I should thank you really. I forgot to set my alarm so at least you kept her from being shorthanded today."

He shrugs, the gray t-shirt he has on strains against his muscles. "I also wanted to make sure you were okay, and I have to fix the washer anyways."

"Well, it was a nice surprise." We finish breakfast all too soon. My heart keeps wanting to watch him like he's some foreign creature, but I already know my heart gets me into too much trouble, so I cast it aside. He's built like a Greek God so it's hard to not look at him.

Jayse places Thora on the floor and stands up. "I should get to the washer. I'll probably have to get the parts if my guess is correct."

"Oh okay," I replied. I try to keep the disappointment out of my voice but it's there. "Well, thank you again." Jayse smiles as he opens the door. He reminds me to take it easy as he leaves.

My apartment feels too quiet without his presence now. It's an odd feeling. Once the table is cleaned up, I head over to my art corner, inspiration hitting me. Jayse is front and center of the inspiration, but when I reach my easel, I realize I left my new canvases in the backseat of my car last night with all the commotion going on. I head upstairs to shower and get dressed before I head down to grab the canvases. As I'm in the shower, I decide to try and wash my hair without irritating the cut. Somehow, I manage to get it done. While I'm combing through my hair, I notice how faded my color is. I meant to get a new hair dye while I was in Atlanta yesterday but I got sidetracked in the art supply store. I never made it to the beauty supply store.

When I started dying my hair bright, off the wall colors it was to calm my soul. A part of me felt like everything had been out of my control. My series of bad decisions had left me feeling at the mercy of every other person in the world. I hated that feeling so I needed something I felt I was in control of. At the time, it was the only thing I could think of to do to give me the feeling of being in control. Now, I look at it, an older, wiser version of myself and I see something that I feel is silly. I've grown into my own person. I stand on my own two feet. I don't need anyone to complete me like I had thought once upon a time. That sense of control is something I feel daily without the crazy hair color. Could it be time for a change?

After I throw my hair into a messy bun, I slip on a pair of glasses and some clothes. Grabbing my keys, as I head out the door and down to my car. To my surprise Jayse is still here. He's humming along to an old country song playing throughout the bottom floor. It makes me smile as I head out to my car. Getting the canvases in and out of my car always seems to be a bit of a task but eventually I get them. When I turned around, I yelp in surprise. Jayse is standing in the doorway, leaning against the frame, wiping his greasy hands on a rag. A chunk of hair has slipped out of his ponytail, hiding a good portion of his face. "What are you up to, Bright Eyes?"

"You mean other than having a heart attack?"

One corner of his mouth quirks up in a smirk. "You know if you were actually taking it easy like you were told to do, then you wouldn't have a heart attack."

I cross my arms over my chest and lean back against my car. "I assumed all of Blue Ridge knew I rarely do what I'm told to do. Granted, it's probably caused more issues in my life than I need, but it's still true."

He pushes away from the door frame and closes the distance between us. "Are these going up?"

"Yeah, but I can carry them."

"Take. It. Easy." Jayse turns away from me, the mint from his breath mixed with the coffee makes me sway on my feet. It's intoxicating. He gathers the canvases in his arms and heads inside. I scurry to catch back up with him. He marches inside, heading straight for my art corner. Briefly, he reaches out and pets Thora. "Hey there, Thora." Once he's placed the canvases in the corner, he turns back towards me. "Anything else you need?"

I shake my head. "Nope, I'm good. Thank you."

Jayse smirks as he passes me. "You are welcome Bright Eyes. Now, take it easy." I roll my eyes, but he's already out the door.

About an hour later, I gather my stuff and headed downstairs. I'm shocked to still hear Jayse banging away on the washer. Instead of heading for my car I head towards the laundry room. Bad decision. A shirtless, sweating Jayse is lying on the floor in all of his glory. I can't see his face because it's hidden by the washer. I'm pretty sure I'm drooling on the floor. Shaking my head, I nudge his thigh with my foot. He pops his head out. Jayse's gray eyes survey me. I don't miss the pause he gives when he sees my purse and keys in hand. "Are you planning on being here all day?"

He cocks his head to the side. "I'm not sure. It looks like it might be a while. I'm going to see if Everett has the parts I need before going over to Atlanta. Why?"

I shrug my shoulders. "I was going to see if you would want lunch. I'm heading out and it'll be a bit before I'm back, but I can bring us lunch when I get back, you know kind of a thank you for last night."

Jayse sits up. "And where do you think you're going?" My eyebrows shoot up at the question. He has no right to ask that. I don't belong to him. As if he can read my mind, he holds up his hands in surrender and says, "I only ask because you are supposed to be taking it easy. Plus, driving isn't really recommended when you have any form of concussion."

"Oh please, I'm fine," I huff out with a roll of my eyes. "I'm just going to Chop Chop to get my hair done."

"That's perfect. I'll drive," he says, as he steps around me, grabbing his shirt off his toolbox. He pulls it over his impressive torso which I'm sad to see go. He goes over to the sink in the corner of the room and washes his hands and splashes water on his face, drying off with a paper towel. When he turns around, he smiles. "Okay, I'm ready."

"You can't be serious."

Jayse smirks and the butterflies take flight in my stomach. I don't think I've seen him smile this much the entire time I've been in Blue Ridge. "Oh, I'm serious, Bright Eyes." He steps around me. I follow behind him and watch as he unhooks his keys from his belt loop. Once he's out the door, he moves past my car and starts to cross the alley. I stop because I think he's overreacting. When he doesn't hear me following, he stops and turns back around. "I said I'd drive."

"And I said I was fine."

He pinches the bridge of his nose. "Stop being stubborn."

My turn to smirk. "Stop overreacting."

"Do you think I'm overreacting, Capri?" I nod my head, but the look in his eyes causes my heart to stutter. His smirk grows into a wolfish grin and the next thing I know he is purposefully striding towards me. His long legs eating up the ground between us. When he reaches me, he doesn't hesitate for even a second before bending down and scooping me up in his arms. I scream in surprise. "This is what overreacting looks like. I was trying to be reasonable, but clearly you don't take well to that. Also, I would have flipped you over my shoulder, but considering you have a concussion, it's not the best idea," I huff and he chuckles as he carries me across the alley, through his backyard, and to his truck. The whole time I act like I'm upset, but really, I can't escape the feeling of how right he feels.

SIX

Jayse

Cleaning up the water on the bottom floor of Capri's building took longer than I anticipated. By the time I get home, I was drenched, from water or sweat, I'm not totally sure. Heading straight for the shower I turn it on full blast and strip down to nothing. The steady stream washes the day away, but I notice that unfamiliar feeling in my chest still lingers. The last thing I expected was for this feeling to reappear. It's been absent for years. Nothing but a hole and echo where my heart once was but it's almost as if I can feel it beating again. Once the house is locked up, I climb in between the cool sheets of my bed with the intention of getting some sleep. However, almost two hours later and I'm still lying in bed, wide awake, watching the ceiling fan rotate above. I can never sleep in complete silence, so I leave the ceiling fan running at night.

Capri's side comments haunt me and every time I close my eyes, I see her sincere, seafoam green eyes. It's obvious she's been through more than her fair share of things. Clearly, she's been hurt before, but that thought is unimaginable to me. How anyone could hurt her...well, it makes my blood boil. Anger is a faithful friend of mine these days, but it's hitting a new level thinking about what she could have possibly been through, how she might have been treated.

Eventually, sleep finds me, but it's once again plagued by nightmares. Only the recurring nightmare has morphed. Capri is trapped in a ring of fire, begging me to help her, to save her, but I'm unable to move. I'm paralyzed by the fear, anxiety and guilt that lives within my body. Her voice is hoarse from the smoke she's taken in and the emotion in her voice is overwhelming. My heart tells me to move forward, to place one foot in front of the other and get to her, to save her. Redeem myself, but my brain has me frozen in place in the middle of an inferno.

Once again, I sit up in my bed, tangled in the sheets. My anxiety at an all-time high, the sheet feels like flames closing in on me, suffocating me from the inside out the way smoke does. I struggle to free myself, once I'm free I stumble out of the bed and my knees hit the floor. Leaning forward I rest my head on the cool wood floor beneath me. My chest feels like there is an elephant sitting on top of it. I struggle to clear my head enough to do the breathing exercises my therapist taught me years ago. Panic grows, constricting the movement of my lungs. Breaths come out in tiny gasps and my head swims in dizziness. This is exactly why I don't let anyone new into my life. This is why I keep my distance at all costs. My nightmares seem to be a forever thing for me, but when it changes...that's not something I'm prepared for.

After some time, everything slows down, the breathing exercises work, and my world turns back to normal. I crawl from my spot on the floor to the chair that sits in the corner of the room. The leather is cool to my skin, and I sigh in relief after the first deep breath, I managed to take. Why had Capri shown up in the damn nightmare? It's ridiculous the way the mind can turn things around.

At some point I must have dozed off, sitting in the chair. The shining moonlight wakes me as it peeks through the slats of the vertical blinds. Stretching my stiff muscles, I stand up. The first thought on my mind is I wonder how Capri made it through the night. Swiftly, I make my way to the kitchen and open the blinds. To my surprise Capri's blinds are still closed so maybe she actually listened and is going to take it easy but just to be safe...

I dress quickly, hopping on my bike. I'm sitting outside of Bee's Batter when Warbee arrives. She jumps with a startle. "Jayse, you scared the daylights out of me?"

"I'm sorry. I just wanted to make sure Capri told you about what happened last night."

Warbee's eyes widen, and I see a thousand questions roll through them. That one look answers the question I had. Capri did not tell her, which means she's probably planning on coming to work which does not qualify as taking it easy. "What happened? Is she okay?" Warbee asks. Concern and protectiveness lacing every word. Warbee really can be a firecracker. I quickly explained what happened and her shoulders ease. "But she's okay?" she asks again.

I nod my head. "Yes, she's fine. She just needs to take it easy."

"Then she will. If she shows up, I'll send her home." Warbee smiles. I turned around and head back towards my bike, feeling like I did a good deed. "Jayse?" I turned back around to Warbee. The streetlights are still on since the sun isn't out yet. Chilly breeze nips at my skin. "Capri has an amazing heart and soul. Be careful with it though. She's more fragile than she seems." Warbee turns around and heads inside her bakery. I stand on the sidewalk, trying to make sense of what I'm feeling. My heart thundered in my chest. There's only one person I can talk to right now. My motorcycle rumbles to life as I take off down the quiet streets.

I'm leaning against my motorcycle when she appears, wiping sleep from her eyes. When she notices me, her eyes widen briefly before a smile takes over her face, completely erasing the stress that was there moments before. "You know, considering we live in the same small town, you go missing for long periods of time."

"I know. I'm sorry," I tell her, as I pull her in for a hug.

"I just got off work and I probably smell like antiseptic." She tries to push me back, but I don't budge.

My laugh fills the silent parking lot, the sun starting to peek up in the clouds. "You forget we used to live together. I've smelled you at your worst."

"Ugh! Shut up! You're horrible." She slaps my chest.

I lean down and smile. "But you love me."

She rolls her eyes, and it instantly reminds me of Capri. Something inside me shifts. "Because we're related. Don't let that ego inflate any more than it already has. So, what brings you around my part of the world, Big Brother?"

Whitney is my younger sister. She's a nurse at the local hospital. Whitney has a knack for helping people when they are at their worst. She also gives the best advice. No one knows me better than her. We have the same chocolate brown hair and stormy gray eyes, but she's petite. "Can't a brother just want to see his sister?"

"Normal brothers...sure. You...never." She raises her eyebrows in suspicion. I shrug my shoulders and she gasps "Oh. My. It has to do with a girl!" Her voice reaches an octave that only dogs can hear. The little jumpy dance she's doing while clapping is another sign that she's clearly lost her mind.

I place my hands on her shoulders to stop her dancing. "I think my ears are bleeding."

"You didn't say no," she says, pointing a finger at me.

"I didn't say yes either, but why are you so excited?"

Whitney comes to stand beside me, leaning against the motorcycle. "Is it wrong that I want to see my brother happy?"

Sighing, I reply, "Not everyone deserves to be happy."

"Bullshit. Everyone does, but not everyone believes that they do. You're one of those tortured souls that doesn't believe you deserve it. You're wrong, you carry your hurt and guilt so close that no one can get through the webs you've weaved unless they have a wrecking ball." Whitney looks up and gives me a small, sad smile. "You aren't supposed to live this way, Jayse. No one wants this for you."

"And no one gets it," I bite back.

She reaches up and slaps the back of my head lightly. "Don't snap at me and yes, we get some of it. We've been watching you for years. I get that you feel like you failed and that you lost more than any of us truly know but no one blames you. Hell, you almost died trying to save them. It's not your fault the roof came down at that point in time."

Moving away from the bike, I shake my head and begin to pace. The panic and anxiety building, eating me up inside once again. "Stop. Just stop."

My sister, who stands a foot shorter than me, comes to stand directly in front of me, blocking my path. Her arms are crossed, and her gray eyes look like a hurricane about to erupt. "No! You came to me because you want tough love. If you wanted someone to tell you it was all okay to keep living like this, you would have gone to Mom and Dad. You're here, so suck it up buttercup."

"Whit…" My voice sounds weak, defeated, lost. It's a plea, but I don't even know what I want.

"Let it go. Stop carrying a burden around that you couldn't help. It's okay to live. You're allowed to live."

Her words pierce my heart, but I'm not sure they'll stay. We've had conversations like this before, but it's never stuck. After a few hours I'll slip back into my pity-party and sulk there. Then again, I've never had someone like Capri. It seems crazy because I don't even know her, but some part of me feels her on a different level. She pulled at my heart strings and now I'm not sure how to navigate.

Whitney steps forward. "That's all I've got for now, Jayse, but try to actually do what I say this time. You deserve this. I'm exhausted so I'm going to go home and get some sleep. I love you. Please, be careful."

I wrap her in my arms and press a kiss to the top of her head. She really does smell like antiseptic, but I'd never tell her that. "Thank you, Whit. I love you."

She heads towards her car but stops just as I'm about to swing my leg over my motorcycle. "Whoever she is. I already like her." Whitney winks before she gets into her car. I wait until her taillights disappear. "I like her, too," I whisper. Almost like I'm breaking all kinds of rules by saying it, but Whitney is right. I need to let it all go.

My mind is made up as I head back into town, stopping by Bee's Batter again. I grab drinks and breakfast for Capri, and I then head back home. I'm shocked to see her blinds are still closed as I come around my house. Anticipation making my feet move a little quicker. After knocking, I hear her moving around inside. When she finally makes it to the door some part of me, I haven't seen in a long time resurfaces. I think I'm actually flirting with her and right now, at this moment, it feels good.

SEVEN

Jayse

Carrying Capri to my truck wasn't my plan but she's so damn stubborn that I didn't have much choice either. However, as I carry her the cinnamon, nutmeg, and clove scent clings to her skin and invades my senses. She smells like all the best scents of autumn and Bee's Batter. I can tell Capri thinks I'm overreacting and maybe I am. There's some part of me that has this undeniable sense of protection where she stands. I barely know her, but I feel this sense of duty towards her and surprisingly I don't mind it. It's been a long time since I felt like I had some sense of purpose. Stepping away from being a firefighter changed my life. I feel like I lost more of myself in one night than I ever knew possible.

Somehow trying to help Capri last night kicked something into perspective for me. However, the nightmare from last night is still haunting me but it feels like a distant memory in her presence. Being around her makes everything else seem to fade away. I forget about a lot of things. Sometimes it's nice to forget. "Here we are," I announce, as we round my house and I see my truck sitting in the driveway.

"Are you going to buckle me up, too?" Her tone is laced with sarcasm. She's adorable when she's sarcastic, but I bite back the laughter I feel building in my chest. Somehow, I don't think laughing at her right now would do me much good.

"Would you like assistance with that?"

Capri huffs and rolls her eyes. "You're being absolutely ridiculous."

"So, you keep saying. Also, it can't be healthy to roll your eyes that much," I tease her. Leaning forward, I open the passenger side door and sit her on her feet. For a moment, she stares at me as if I've grown extra heads before shaking her head and climbing inside.

I round the truck and climb inside with her. The cab of my truck smells like wood and mint mixed with all things Capri. It catches me off guard at first, but after a few deep breaths it grows on me. The smells mix well actually. She looks over at me. "You should really warn people."

My eyebrows knit together in confusion. "Warn people about what?"

She nods her head and I'm captivated by the way the sunlight is framing her face right now. It's impossible to turn away from. "That you actually have three sides."

"Oh, I do, do I?" I rub my hands together in anticipation. "Please, tell me what the third side is, because I thought I only had two."

Capri rests her head on the seat and rolls it to look at me. "Caveman."

I don't even attempt to fight back the laughter that bursts out of me. It eats up the silence that was in the truck moments before. Capri's face flushes and her eyes dance in amusement, but she never cracks a smile. I have to give her credit for that. "Is it the hair? Is that what gave you cavemen vibes?"

"Oh no, not the hair. Just the fact that you scooped me up and carried me to your truck. It's such a caveman thing to do and you admitted that if it wasn't for the concussion, you would have thrown me over your shoulder. You do realize we're in the twenty-first century and acting like a caveman is no longer necessary?"

I nod my head. "I do indeed, but whoever said it wasn't necessary has never met the likes of you, Capri Owens. You're so stubborn it takes a caveman to try and get through that overly thick head of yours."

Silence falls between us, and we stare at each other. It almost feels as if we're having a staring contest. Neither blinks nor looks away, at least until she dies laughing and the sound of it hits me square in the gut. It's an unexpected reaction as my insides curl in on themselves. I haven't felt this feeling in years. "Okay, you might be right about that."

"Considering how the last twenty-four hours have gone I'd say there is no might in that verdict." Capri reaches over and nudges my shoulder.

"Would you mind if I roll down my window?" Her question is so quietly asked, that I barely hear the words she speaks. It's almost as if she's scared to ask.

I hit the automatic button on the passenger side window. "You never have to ask. You can adjust it how you'd like from your side."

She looks over at me, those seafoam green eyes full of curiosity. "Thank you." As we roll up to a stop sign, I watch as she takes a deep breath. "I just love this time of year, don't you?"

There's a loaded question. She doesn't even know what she's asked but my heart sinks. Lost in the pit of fiery flames, the very ones that have consumed my entire damn life. "Yeah, I used to," I admit quietly. I feel her intriguing eyes on me, but I keep my own straight ahead on the road. We reach Chop Chop shortly after. Capri never asks what I meant by my comment. I'm thankful for that, but I know she's smart and she knows there's a story behind it. I can feel the curiosity coursing through her veins. The only reason I think she won't ask is because she has a story, too, and I don't think she wants to share it yet. "Here we are," I announce, as I pull into a parking spot a few feet down from the salon.

"Thank you. If you want to leave me here, I can walk down and get a ride from Warbee later."

Quickly, I climb out of the truck and rush to the passenger side. The passenger side door opens just as I reach it. "I brought you and I intend to take you back."

Capri's eyes narrow as she studies me. Finally, she sighs. "This will probably take a while."

I lean forward like I'm about to let her in on a secret. "I'm a patient man. I can wait."

When I pull back, I see a thousand questions rolling through her eyes. Eventually, she nods and climbs out of the truck. "I'll see you in a bit then."

She heads for the salon, and I watch as she leaves. My eyes can't seem to leave her. Something about her has pulled me in and I can't escape, but I'm not sure I want to since this is the first time, I've felt like I'm breathing since that night. I close the door and climb back into the truck. The hardware store is only a few blocks, within walking distance for sure, but I'm not sure how much I'll end up buying and dragging it down the street might not be the best way.

Once I'm parked again, I head inside. This store is my own personal version of a candy store. More than likely, I should have a chaperone because I always spend way too much money and buy things, I have no need for at the moment. Everett is behind the counter and greets me as I enter. He's worked here since high school. Now, he helps run it and eventually he'll own it. It's a family-owned business. Everett is the closest thing I have to a best friend. Well, he's the closest thing I even have to a friend. We grew up together and if anyone knows me...it's him. His sandy blonde hair is buzzed to his head and his brown eyes are always friendly. "Jayse, how's it going?"

I walk over to the counter and shake his hand, just like I always do. "Pretty good. How are you?"

He nods his head. "It's been really busy. The store has been packed. I can't seem to keep certain things in stock. I've been ordering trucks more than once a week. Cayley has been a handful too. Terrible twos and all."

Everett is a single father now. His wife, Dianna, passed away giving birth to their little girl during their first year of marriage. Everett was devastated. He'd had a crush on Whitney for years until he met Dianna. Losing her was one of the hardest things I've seen him go through. I only managed to watch his downward spiral from afar because I was too lost in my own shit to actually be there. "That's great about the store. Sorry that Cayley has been a bit of a handful, but I'm sure she'll grow out of it."

"So, I heard a little rumor."

Oh, this can't be good. News is a sport around this small town. News becomes gossip and travels at the speed of light. Sometimes, it's a good thing but other times it's a curse. "This can't be good."

Everett chuckles. "You know how it goes in Blue Ridge." He gives me an apologetic smile and a shrug of his shoulders.

"Well, I guess let me hear it since I'm not going to be able to escape it."

"You and Capri Owens?" he asks. Everett doesn't come across nosey, just genuinely interested.

I sigh. "It's not like that...at all. I just helped her out and now I'm working in Clark's building which is why I'm here."

Everett laughs again. "Smooth change of subject, but I will accept. Let's find what you need."

Capri said it'd take a while before she was done at Chop Chop, but I ended up spending at least forty-five minutes in Schmidt's Handy Dandy Hardware. Once Everett and I get everything loaded, I head back down to Chop Chop. I don't see any sign of Capri, so I get out with the intention of going inside but then I spot her sitting in a chair, nose in a magazine and hair wrapped in a towel. Quickly, I climb back into the truck and rest my head. The autumn breeze blows through the truck and my eyelids fall closed as I drift off to sleep.

I don't know how much time has passed, but I wake up as the passenger side door opens. I'm still half asleep so it takes me a moment to realize that caramel colored hair beauty standing there looking at me is Capri. "Are you okay there?"

My hands rub my eyes and I look again and sure enough her seafoam green eyes are still staring at me. "Yeah, you just look...different."

She picks up a strand and examines it. "Yeah, it's been a long time since I had a color of hair that's this close to my natural."

"I like it."

Her eyes dart up to mine and a flush fills her cheeks. "Me, too. So, are you ready to go?"

"Yeah, but I have one more idea before we head back."

Capri drops her head back on the head rest. "I don't like surprises."

I look over and wink at her as I put the truck in reverse. "You'll like this one."

EIGHT

Capri

Surprises are not for me. I've never had a good "surprise" in my life so call me crazy but when Jayse said he had an idea...well, it felt like another word for surprise. Especially, since he won't tell me anything about what's going on or what we're doing. Agitation grows within my body and I'm finding it more difficult to sit still. A part of me wants to jump from this moving truck and run for the hills, but somehow, I know that's a bad idea.

Jayse's eyes cut towards me. I can feel them. "Would you please try to relax?"

"I am relaxed." My tone comes out in a bite and proves I'm not at all relaxed like I'm claiming to be. Then there's the fact that my leg hasn't stopped bouncing since he mentioned his idea.

His chuckle annoys me. Earlier, I thought his chuckle was cute and endearing but now it's just pissing me off. "Yeah, you seem super relaxed."

I look at him. Normally, he's the one with tense muscles and a jaw locked so tight that even a crowbar couldn't pry it apart, but it's like we've switched roles. Don't get me wrong, when I first arrived in Blue Ridge, I was very much like him. Constantly, tense, so much so that my entire body ached for months from it. However, as time went along, I realized I was safe here, tucked away in this small town in the mountains. "I told you I don't like surprises."

"I never called it a surprise," he comments, flashing me a brief smirk before turning back to the road in front of us.

Sighing, I reply, "An idea that the other person has no clue about is just another word for surprise."

Jayse pulls into a parking place in front of Burger Hop. A quick glance at the clock on the dash of his truck tells me we've only been driving for approximately seven minutes. It feels more like seven hours. "Do you want to come in?"

"Are you staying here for a while?"

He shakes his head. Stray chunks of hair slip from the hair tie. I watch as his arms reach up and set the chocolate strands free. "No, I'm just grabbing us some food then I'll be back out."

"You didn't have to get me food again," I tell him.

His broad shoulders rise with a shrug. "I know, but I wanted to."

We stare at each other for a fleeting moment. I remember he asked me a question. "I'll wait." Jayse nods his head once and hops out of the truck. I watch as he heads inside. Most of the time he keeps his head down, but every head in the area turns to watch him. Once he disappears inside the restaurant, all of those curious eyes turn to me. I try to hunch down farther into the seat but there's no escape from them. Something tells me this isn't Jayse's normal which makes me curious what exactly is going on here. I may not know much about most of the people in this town because I'm not from here originally and I don't listen to much gossip, but I have noticed that my broody neighbor spends the majority of his time alone.

Jayse reappears with a bright red bag of food and a drink holder with two large cups sitting in it. I pop my door open, and he heads my way. "Here we go. Dinner for two," he playfully says. His tone is light and teasing but there is a tension lurking in his eyes. I must admit he's good and plays off the things that bother him, but I think he's aware that he's being watched and he's uncomfortable because of it. "Are you good?" he asks, and I nod before he shuts the door and walks around the back of the truck and climbs back inside. The smell of juicy hamburgers and hot French fries fill the cab of the truck and my stomach growls in hunger. Jayse looks at me and we burst out laughing. Laughter takes us both over for some unknown reason and the tension eases. It takes a moment for it to subside, and we dry our eyes and Jayse backs out of the parking spot.

The country radio plays quietly as we head towards the outskirts of town. Anxiety fills me once more. Anxiety is something I've become better at controlling. Normally, it doesn't affect me so much, but right now, I'm struggling. "Where are we going?"

"I told you it's a surprise."

I shake my head vigorously. "No, you said it was an idea. You plainly said it wasn't a surprise." My tone must sound harsh. Jayse is turning us down one of the old dirt back roads. Blue Ridge has plenty, but I've never been one to explore on my own.

Jayse chuckles. "Would you just trust me?"

Trust. There is something I don't give out easily. I used to give my trust away like candy on Halloween, but I learned, and I learned the hard way. Trust has to be earned and it's not an easy thing to earn. You can't just throw it at a handsome face or pretty words. Memories from my life before Blue Ridge start to flood my mind and my chest constricts tightly. Breathing becomes difficult. All I can think is not here, not now, I haven't felt panic growing within me in a couple of years. Right after I arrived it happened often, usually when I was alone and felt like he might have found me, but those thoughts and feelings have left me since then and so had the overwhelming feeling of panic. I don't want to do this in front of Jayse. My eyes squeeze shut, and I try to calm myself but it's not working. I gasp and I feel the truck yank towards the side of the road.

I keep my eyes shut to try and help the growing panic. When the passenger side door of the truck is yanked open, I'm startled. My eyelids fly open and Jayse is standing in front of me. "Capri, you need to breathe. You're having a panic attack." I shake my head, unable to speak. Jayse quickly moves the food and drinks from my hands, undoes the seatbelt and pulls me from the truck. He puts me on my feet, but my legs are useless, and I wobble. He wraps an arm around my waist to steady me, the other soothingly moves my hair back from my face. "Just breathe, Capri. Focus on me and breathe."

After a few moments, things started to return to normal in my body. Jayse's stormy gray eyes meet mine. I feel the flush of embarrassment rush through me, and I look away. Jayse's fingers rest under my chin and urge me to look back at him. "It was just a slight panic attack."

"Yeah, I used to have them often," I admit quietly.

His head tips to the side and his hair falls over one side of his face. My fingers itch to move it and see if they feel as silky as they look. "If you ever want to talk, I'll be happy to listen."

I take a step back and stare at him, studying him from a different view. His eyes are lingering in the distance between us. I hold my breath in the moment. Do I trust him, or do I walk away? I know what I should do and then I know what I want to do. "Let's just say, my past is a bit complicated."

Jayse's hand comes up to scratch at the five o'clock shadow coming in on his jaw. "I think that can be said for a lot of us."

"This is different." I can feel myself folding in on me. Closing off from him and the rest of the world. Adding another layer of brick to the already impossibly high wall of defense I've built around my heart. I'm not so sure it can withstand another crack let alone a full break. "You wouldn't understand."

He takes a step back, leans against his truck and stares at me. His eyes open and honest, all guards down. It's the first time his eyes have ever looked...vulnerable. "You might be surprised."

"Would I?" My tone has a bite to it. Jayse doesn't deserve the attitude, but it's my go to defense mechanism. A chilly autumn breeze blows around us. The leaves rustle in the trees surrounding us. I wrap my arms around myself, to fight off the chill or to lock myself back away, I'm not sure.

Jayse's eyes grow colder and close to a glare. "Yeah, you would. Do you think I live my life like this for the hell of it? Because it's fun? No, I have a history, too, and trust me when I say it's not pretty. It's actually about as ugly as this part of my body," he says, as he points to the angry scars that cover a good portion of his body from what I can tell. His voice grows louder with each word. I flinch with each one. He must notice, because he turns around and rests his hands on the truck and hangs his head. "I'm sorry, I didn't mean to raise my voice."

His apology stings. Maybe it shouldn't, but to flinch because someone raised their voice in a heated moment...well, it's just another reminder of my past and how it has changed me. "It's fine."

"No, it's not. I could probably guess some of your past, but I don't like to assume things about people."

"Why not? The rest of the town does." Without realizing it, I've taken two steps towards him. The distance between us is growing smaller.

He chuckles darkly, it doesn't sound like his other laughs. This one is different. Laced with sadness and sarcasm. "Yeah, that one I do know. It's the main reason why I don't assume things."

The way his broad shoulders sag and he shakes his head in disgust makes me want to close the distance completely and wrap my arms around his waist. Some part of me knows how foolish that is. I know better. I've tried and tried and tried to make things work when they aren't meant to. Relationships aren't in the cards for me. I vowed to never need anyone again, but there's this invisible thread pulling me towards Jayse. It holds me captive, unable to go too far. I watch him when no one else knows, amazed by how graceful he is. My ears could hear the sound of his voice in a room full of noise because I listened so intently to every word he said in my presence throughout my time in Blue Ridge. This invisible thread won't let me keep my vow. Closing my eyes, I take a deep breath and dissolve the space between us. "For the record, I don't assume things. I don't know your story or history. Gossip was never something I listened to."

He looks at me from the corner of his eye before standing back up. His eyes leave mine as he stares across the road into the trees beyond. "I've made mistakes and in a town this size everyone knows them. I carry my own guilt with me on a daily basis, but I also carry this town's blame with me."

My hand reaches out and wraps around his bicep. "That can't be true, Jayse. The town loves you. Everyone calls on you when something breaks."

"Because they need something fixed, not because they need me."

His broken and defeated tone pulls at my heartstrings. "You save the day for every person who calls you."

He hangs his head once more and I can feel the sadness coming off him in waves. It's drowning me just standing next to him, so I can't even imagine what he feels. Is it possible that Jayse could understand my pain as much as I could understand his? "I don't always save the day."

"Tell me one time you didn't."

He turns towards me, but the look in his eyes knocks the air right out of me. "The night I got these scars, I didn't save a damn thing that night."

NINE

Jayse

The words taste like acid on my tongue. In some ways I wish they were acid. Right now, I need them to burn my tongue right off because this wasn't part of the plan. I don't talk about that night. I never will and certainly not with Capri, but then something about her is different. Something draws me to her. I'm unable to escape from her. It feels like something in her soul recognizes something in mine and we can't break away from one another. Her seafoam green eyes beg to give her understanding. She's asking for my past without saying the words. I read in her eyes. I feel it coming off her body in waves. She's ready to take on the burden of my past, or at least, she thinks she is. In reality no one is ready to take on that burden.

I want her past, but it's not an even trade. For me to ask her for something I'm not willing to give is completely unfair. My throat feels like mud, my tongue like cotton and my lungs feel as if all the pressure in the world is on them. Capri, not knowing my past, still looking at me as if I can be a hero, I'm not, it's something I'm willing to lose. For all of my life I wanted one thing to be a firefighter...to be a hero. In my mind, they were one in the same. I thought it was my destiny, but then that night happened, and my dream was shattered like broken glass. Taken in a split moment as the flames ate away at the house and my skin.

My hand reaches out, in search of the one thing that has felt like an anchor the past few weeks. Ever since I stepped foot inside Bee's Batter and got close to Capri, she feels like she keeps my feet on the ground. She's gravity and I'm just another planet lost in the orbit of rotation. I'm the ship lost at sea, but she's my anchor keeping me calm and steady in the eye of a storm. It's silly because I barely know her, yet it feels like I've known her my whole life.

As if she can feel my hesitation, her hand wraps around mine and she pulls it towards her. My palm comes to rest on her cheek. She barely flinches but I still catch it. I ache to correct the wrongs that have been done to her. "I want your past. I want to know why you flinch. I want to know why you keep everyone at a distance. I don't deserve to know. I don't deserve your past, but I want it. The worst part is I can't even tell you why I want it."

She sighs. Her skin feels like silk against the roughened skin of my hand. "If you want it, then all you have to do is ask. Maybe, I'm being foolish because I've worked so hard to leave it behind, and to become a different version of myself. Promising myself I'll never let anyone in again, but with you...it's different."

"I can't ask for it because if I do then you have the right to ask for mine and that's not something I can give to you, Capri." I pull my hand from the warmth and silky softness of her and take a step back. I rake my fingers through my hair roughly as I turn away from her. The last image I see is her seafoam green eyes, widened in shock and laced in hurt. "This was a mistake. I shouldn't have brought you out here. I shouldn't have gotten involved in your life or tried to bring you into mine. We should go." Guilt eats at me, devouring me from the inside out. I'm the worst kind of human. I keep failing at every turn. Turning around and forgetting about Capri is the best thing I can do for her, and the best thing I can do for the memories that will forever be a part of my DNA.

"Jayse..." she whispers. Her voice breaks and it tears at me, ripping my already weakened soul into shreds.

I shake my head. "I can't. I know you don't understand, but it's me, Capri, not you. That sounds like a lame excuse, but it's the honest truth."

Capri hasn't moved from her spot as I make my way around the truck. Her voice stops me in my tracks. "I ran away from my home when I was sixteen with a guy on a motorcycle named Billy, not because I loved him, but because as bad as Billy and his crowd were, my father was much worse. He was a raging alcoholic with substance abuse issues, and a temper as high as the Empire State Building. He liked to use fists and kicks instead of words when he was in a stupor. When he wasn't doing drugs, he was dealing them. The place I called home, a trailer that was barely standing, was normally full of drunk men, drugs, and half-dressed women paying off debts owed to the club. Running away seemed like the answer at the time. The funny thing about running is that once you start...you can't stop."

Her words dance in the air, but they aren't beautiful. They're tragic. Her life shouldn't have been like this. "Capri, you don't have to tell me this. I didn't ask."

"You didn't ask, so I'm volunteering the information." She moves to stand directly across from me. The truck is between us, but even from here I can feel her, the sincerity that makes up her soul and the kindness that swims in her eyes.

"What about your mom?"

A sad smile. A sarcastic laugh. Silence falls between us for a moment as Capri cuts her eyes to the side. "She got out. Left my father and I and started a new life. A picture-perfect life with a picture-perfect family."

I can't even imagine what that must have felt like for her. The things she must have seen...it turns my stomach. "I'm sorry."

She shrugs her tiny shoulders. "Shit happens. So, I left with Billy and never looked back. He belonged to a different Motorcycle club in a different town. They were a rival to my father's club, so that meant that my dad wouldn't cross their territory lines. Not that he cared that I was gone. For him, it was one less mouth to feed, one less body taking up space in his place. I stayed with Billy for a while. He was a pretty face with a lot of charm, and he knew it. He cheated a lot, but I wasn't in love with him so, to be honest, I didn't care. Billy was a way out of the trailer park for me. An escape from my father and the life he chose for himself."

The sinking feeling in my gut tells me that Billy isn't the end of her story. "Why do I feel like Billy isn't the end of your story?"

Capri looks at me, Her eyes open, completely unguarded and sincere. A small smile graces her face, but there's sadness wrapped around it, and I want to eliminate the truck between us and pull her into my arms. Protect her from whatever else life has thrown at her. "Not even close to the end. Billy was just the beginning." Capri shakes her head as if she can't believe she was once young and naive. We've all been there, but I can tell that the decisions made during that time are weighing on her. "After Billy...I ran to a new city where I knew no one. I was working as a waitress in this old truck stop when Eddy showed up. He drove a semi and was in the diner at least once a week. There was something about him that just screamed danger and there's something within me that can't resist that. We moved way too fast and the next thing I knew, I was living on the outskirts of Las Vegas on some dirt road in a little one-bedroom shack with a car that barely ran. Eddy made good money, which was good since I wasn't allowed to work, but he failed to mention that he spent all of his money on drugs and booze. Eddy was the younger version of my father. He'd take his anger out on me when he needed a fix. So, one night after he finally got his fix and was passed out, I ran, and I never looked back. I made it all the way to Dallas, Texas."

For whatever reason, I've made my way back around the truck so that I'm standing next to her. I study her profile. I would have never guessed this was her past. A part of me knew it wasn't perfect, but I never considered this.

She sighs. "This is the last part. I managed to get a job at a department store in one of the malls. Kurt Cunning walked in. In Dallas he's basically royalty. He was born with a silver spoon in his mouth, the eldest child of one of the largest oil companies in the area. Old oil money is what my coworker told me. I watched avidly as he strode into the men's area of the fancy store and was fitted for suits. Charisma and sex oozed off him, drowning me. He was cocky, but he could afford to be. It's a luxury most of us will never know. The man doing the fitting ran out of pins, so he hollered for more. I was the closest, so I helped him out. Kurt noticed me. Afterwards, he wined and dined me. Bought me every pretty thing you could imagine. Showed me a lavish life, something I never thought my trailer park self would know. When he asked me to marry him, it was with a seven-carat diamond. Kurt was not a man you said no to, but the thing is I was completely in love with him. I wanted to marry him, and we did. He moved me into a mansion. Custom-built with land everywhere. Luxury cars at my disposal and all the money to buy all the things. Or, at least, that's how it seemed at first. It changed pretty quickly. Kurt didn't have a drug or alcohol problem. He never cheated, that I knew about, but he had a temper and a control issue. He wanted everything done and in a certain way exactly when he said it. When he didn't get his way the abuse started, both verbal and physical. Eventually, I got to the point where I just couldn't do it anymore." Her voice breaks and tears silently stream down her face, as she stares at the setting sun in the distance.

Without a second thought, I reach forward and wrap and arm around her shoulders. Her head comes to rest on my shoulder. I can feel the shuttering as she cries. Pulling her into me seems like the only reasonable choice so I do. She buries her face into my shirt and cries. I don't know how long we stand there but when she pulls away, I can see she's about to apologize. I don't want her to be sorry for her past. It's shaped her into who she is today, and the person in front of me seems quite extraordinary. As I shake my head to stop her from speaking, one of my hands snakes up to tangle into her newly colored hair. I don't think... because I can't. If I stop to think then I'll talk myself out of this and right now it's the only thing I want. When the guilt comes tomorrow, I'll take it like I deserve it and move on, but right now, I need Capri. My lips collide with hers in a hurried, but passionate kiss. It brings my whole body to life. The kiss is unlike anything I've experienced before. Her nails rake against my back, shoulders, chest and biceps. Each trace of fingernails leaves me breathless and wanting more. When we finally break apart, I can't see, think, or breathe straight. When I meet her eyes, I know it was worth it.

TEN

Capri

Jayse. He's the only thing I can see in this moment. The only thing that I can feel. He's consuming me. I confessed my life's worth of bad decisions and he devoured them. Accepted them. Yet, he still looked at me with that amazement lurking in the stormy gray of his eyes. Jayse looks at me as if I have more to offer than I believe I do. He makes me believe I can be better than I have. We barely know each other but I feel him in every fiber of my being. It's almost as if he's drawn me to Blue Ridge. It's not possible, but these last few days it's felt like it.

The memory of our kiss lingers in my mind. My lips can still feel the pressure and roughness of his. His taste is still there on my tongue. The feel of his hands tangled in my hair. It's all still there like it just happened. A night of sleep has done nothing to change my mind, I'm not sure about his mind though. What will he feel this morning?

It's obvious he carries a burden of guilt with him. It lingers in his bones and eats at his soul. I've always seen that. One of my art teachers in high school told me that as an artist I had an eye for sensing others pain. I didn't really think that was true until Jayse. From the moment I laid eyes on him, I could sense it. Regret. Grief. Guilt. It oozed off him the way some men oozed sex appeal. Jayse was trapped in turmoil. Broody and sullen. He kept the world at arm's length, something I completely understood. That day I couldn't take my eyes off him. He was standing in his backyard, cutting wood, shirtless. Sweat glistened off his bare skin as the sunlight found ways to hit him through the trees overhead. He looked like something out of a movie, except he held much more within him than a pretty face and good body.

Rolling over in my bed, I stare at the ceiling above me. My hands itch. The sign that I need to drown them in paint. That incessant need to do something more. The stark white ceiling above me is a blank canvas in my mind. I have a few hours to kill before I head into work. Warbee had called yesterday afternoon at some point. When I got back home last night and finally checked my voicemails, she had told me I was only allowed to work half a day today. A part of me wanted to call and tell her I'd be at the bakery bright and early, but it was late, and I knew it would be useless.

After Jayse and I kissed, we climbed back into the truck, and he continued down the dirt road to a small hill. We collected the food which had gone cold, but was still as delicious and sat on top of the hill and watched the world around us. It was quiet and peaceful. Looking out over the trees, it felt like it was just Jayse and I in the world. When we arrived back at his house, he had walked me to my door, pressed a light kiss to my forehead, and then disappeared into the night. I didn't bother to turn on the lights in my apartment as I rushed to the windows that faced the alley. I watched as he slowly made his way back to his house. The way his body seemed to be turned in on itself...I could tell he was having conflicting emotions. I still didn't know his past. I wish I did. There was a part of me that had hoped he would share with me once I started talking about my own, but he didn't. Sure, I could ask Warbee or even Teaganne. Blue Ridge is small and even Jayse said the entire town knew his past, but I'd rather hear it from him.

A knock on my front door causes both Thora and I to jump. Quickly, I climb out of bed and make my way down the stairs. I take a moment to look out of the peep hole and see Jayse standing there. Quickly, I spin around to look at my reflection in the mirror. My hair looks similar to a bird's nest. There are indents on my face from where I had slept in the same position for so long. Underneath my eyes are puffy from sleep. Oh well, there's no helping this right now I realize when another knock comes from the door. Taking a deep breath, I pull it open. Jayse's scent rushes in and invades every sense I have. It really should be illegal to smell so good. Concentration isn't possible with him around. His hair is down and loose, looking a bit windblown which makes me think he's been on his motorcycle. "Good morning, Bright Eyes."

An airy laugh escapes me and I'm not quite sure what that's all about. "Good morning to you, too."

Jayse holds up a bag of greasy food with a smile large enough to put his dimples on full display. "More food?"

"You need to eat," he comments, as he moves around me to enter the apartment. Thora comes rushing over towards him. Her purrs fill the silence of the apartment.

"I do eat."

I watch as he sits the bag down on my tiny table and scoops up Thora who is rubbing against his legs. "How are you this morning, Beautiful?"

Laughter bubbles out of me once more. "I never would have guessed you had such a soft spot for cats."

His broad shoulders shrug and he smiles. "I like all animals just about. By the way, I didn't mean the food comment like that. Confession time…. I don't like to eat alone. It's why I'm never in any of the restaurants in town. I'll get food to go, but I won't go in and sit down. I don't know why, but I just don't feel comfortable."

A smile hits my face. There's something about Jayse that seems fearless and indestructible, so to hear him confess something like this has caught me off guard, but it also makes my heart flutter. He trusted me enough to let me know something about him that I'm pretty sure most people don't know. "I would have never guessed that."

"So, give me a confession." He winks. Sometimes, I don't think he realizes how devastatingly handsome he truly is.

As I head towards the table, he walks around and pulls my chair out for me. I can honestly say that this has never been done for me before, but I don't hate it. "You mean, more confessions than what I gave you yesterday."

"Okay, that's fair." He takes a seat with Thora in his lap. He pulls out two bottles of chocolate milk and two breakfast sandwiches from Burger Hop's breakfast menu. They are so good, but messy as hell. I'm a little embarrassed to eat this in front of him. "How about something you've always wanted to do?"

Of course, he asks the question right as I take an overly large bite of the breakfast sandwich. He watches with an amused smile as I try to chew and quietly as possible. Finally, I'm able to answer the question. It's the easiest thing I've ever been asked. "Have you seen Princess Diaries?"

"The movie?" I nod my head. "Yeah, I have."

My eyebrows shoot up in surprise. "I'm impressed."

He laughs, a full belly laugh. It's a deep rumble that causes goosebumps to coat my skin. "Don't be too impressed. I have a sister in case you didn't know." I did know that, but we'll pretend I didn't. "So, what about Princess Diaries?"

I've never admitted this to anyone before, so it feels odd to even say it out loud. "Do you remember the scene where Mia and her mom have the canvas full of balloons that are filled with different colors of paint, and they throw darts at them?"

His eyes shine with knowledge. Jayse already knows where I'm going with this. "I do remember."

Sighing, I admit, "I've always wanted to do that."

Jayse turns around and surveys the room. "Well, you're an artist and you definitely have enough space so why haven't you?"

"I wasn't sure how to rig it up honestly. Plus, I kind of suck at throwing darts. I feel like I'd miss more of the balloons than I'd pop."

"It does seem like it'd be more fun with someone to help as well." I can see mischief in his eyes, but I don't even bother to ask. "Do you work today?" he asks.

"Yeah, half of the day anyways. Just this afternoon until closing. Warbee is still requesting I take it easy," I tell him, my eyes narrowing into a glare that I don't feel.

Jayse holds up his large hands in surrender. My eyes are drawn to the scars on the inside of his palm. I had never noticed them before. I think back to all of the times he's touched me, and I realize it's never been with this hand. Before I can think about it, my hand reaches forward and locks with his. He flinches. "Capri…"

"Stop hiding it. Stop hiding from me. I didn't even realize your palm was burned like this."

"Good. I make it a point to not touch people with it." He looks away from our clasped hands in disgust.

I shake my head, unable to understand. "Why?"

Abruptly, Jayse releases my hand and stands up. "I need to get to work. I'll talk to you later but make sure you take it easy." He pauses beside my chair. I hold my breath. Uncertainty controls my body right now, but just when I think there's no hope he leans down and presses a kiss to the top of my head. Calmly and quietly, he leaves. When the door shuts behind him, I turn to look at it. Why? I don't know. It's not as if it holds any answers but it feels like a part of me just left with Jayse. I just want to ease his pain that he won't even admit he carries. It's easy to see if you know what to look for. Clearly, everything has to do with how his body got burned, but I also know he's not going to talk until he's ready.

My hands itch as I stand up from the table and make my way to the blank canvas in the corner of the living room. Inspiration hits me like a tidal wave. The paints are calling my name. I grab the remote and turn on the music and lose myself in a different world until it's time to get to work. Even from here, I can feel his eyes on me. He's hidden by the trees in his backyard, but the heat is there. Pushing the thought away I go to work on something completely different from my normal.

Stephanie Nichole

ELEVEN

Capri

From the moment I walked into Bee's Batter, it has been nonstop. There were a few months where we worried about business. The Sip and Smack was new, and it seemed the owner, Fran, was out to personally take down Warbee. Thankfully, that didn't last, but today is like no other. The closest parking space I could find was four blocks away, so I ended up parking in the alley behind the bakery, in front of Warbee. When I joined Warbee and Jolie behind the counter, I had no idea my day was going to be like this. I know Jayse and Warbee said to take it easy, but it's not possible on a day like this.

Once we close for the night, I send Warbee and Jolie home since they both worked all day long. I could manage the clean up on my own. They both kept trying to insist on staying and helping, but it only seemed fair to me. Jolie heads out first and I pull the front door closed and lock it from the inside. Warbee studies me with worried eyes. "What?" I ask.

She shakes her head. "I just feel horrible leaving you here with a possible concussion. You're supposed to be taking it easy, and I know today definitely didn't fall under the category of easy."

I release my hair from the ponytail it's been in and shake it out. "I promise I'm okay. Jayse overreacted a bit. He was incredibly sweet, so I don't want to be too much of a, well you know what, about it but I was fine. "

"He just always wants to help people. Ever since I have known him, that's who he's been. I remember when we were kids...he'd go around the neighborhoods and mow lawns and rake leaves for the elderly. Jayse never charged them a dime; he just did it. The gossip musketeer's mother had always loved gardening, it's how they all got flower names, but when she got older, and her arthritis set in she couldn't garden anymore. She'd just sit on her porch and stare at the yard. She always looked so sad. One day, Jayse marched onto her property and started taking out all the dead flowers. She yelled at him and threatened him with her walker. It really was funny, but once he explained he was going to plant new flowers for her, she calmed down. After that, he'd show up in her yard, every year, like clockwork and plant fresh flowers for her garden."

My heart feels like a kid rushing down the stairs on Christmas morning. The pitter patter makes no sense. "Wow."

"Yeah, as soon as he was old enough, he volunteered at the local animal shelter. He went with his mom to the nursing homes here and surrounding areas to deliver Christmas gifts. Jayse could probably have gone to the NFL like Rocker, but he didn't want that. He went to work at a local ranch during high school and as soon as he graduated, he signed up to become a firefighter," Wabee explains. She pauses and her eyes get a sad look at them at the mention of Jayse's firefighting days.

I hold up my hand to keep her from telling me his story. "I'd like to know his past. Actually, it's killing me not knowing what he's been through, but I want to hear it from him, when he's ready to talk about it."

Warbee's head falls to the side as she studies me. "You like him, don't you, Capri?"

There's the million-dollar question. The answer is simple or at least it should be but it's not an easy answer for me. Someone with my past and everything I've been through often has a difficult time opening up, letting someone in. I also made myself a promise not to repeat the same mistakes. Do I think Jayse is like my exes? No, I don't, but I've been wrong before. "I could."

"You could if you let yourself…" Warbee sighs, and leans over the counter. "I've been there in a sense. Look I don't know your past fully, but I could probably guess some of it. I do know his past and I can tell you that under that broody, silent shell is an amazing person who is worth the shot. He seems to have taken a liking to you and for Jayse that's huge. He hasn't let anyone behind his walls in a long time." Warbee stands back up and gives me a hug. She heads through the kitchen, and I follow her until she hits the back door. Before she opens it, she turns back around to me. "You deserve to be happy, too. You and Jayse have a lot of the same qualities and I think the two of you could be good for one another. Promise me you'll just think about it."

I nod my head. "I promise. Now, please go home and rest." Warbee leaves and locks the door behind her. I walk back up to the front and turn on the music. It's just too quiet without it. An hour passes and almost everything is clean. I'm in the kitchen when a sound echoes over the music and rings out through the bakery. I stop, holding my breath, and listen again. No more sounds come from the front. It could have just been my mind playing tricks on me or something as simple as a bird hitting the window. I continue cleaning up when suddenly the music goes silent. It's so quiet you could hear a pin drop. Unable to breathe or make a sound, I wait. As quickly as possible, I make my way over to the counter and grab one of the knives. My heart races as I start to make my way to the wooden swinging door that separates the kitchen from the front of the bakery. I'm almost there when the lights go out. The moment the darkness takes over my heart stops. Something is wrong. Very, very wrong.

My cell phone vibrates in the front pocket of the apron I'm still wearing. I want to answer it, but I'm afraid that if someone is in fact inside the bakery with me, they will hear me. However, the annoying vibrating noise my phone is currently making is no help. The noise could easily lead someone to me as well. As the vibrating stops, I pull the phone from my pocket. Jayse's name is on the screen. I'm torn with what to do when a text message comes through, lighting up my phone again.

Jayse: *Are you okay? The power is out for most of the town, and I don't see your car at your apartment.*

My chest heaves in relief. I'm completely overreacting. I quickly dial Jayse's number. "Capri, are you okay?"

"Yeah, I'm at the bakery. I thought someone was inside with me when the lights went out." My voice shakes and wobbles. I hate how weak I sound right now. That feeling of tears pricking the back of my eyes and emotion filling my throat, making it difficult to breathe comes over me. Anxiety rises up from the pit of my stomach and storms through the rest of my body.

I hear Jayse rustling around on the end of the line. "There's a big storm brewing. I think it might have something to do with the outage. I'm coming to get you."

I shake my head no, but realize he can't actually see me. "No, I'm fine. I'm almost done here then I'll be heading home."

"Capri, I'm still coming so just wait for me if you finish before I make it." The line goes dead, and he is gone. My heart thunders in my chest. I turn around and grip the counter. My knuckles white from the strength behind that grip, trying to use everything within me to fight back the paralyzing anxiety I'm currently feeling. Memories come to me so quickly, I can't distinguish what is past or present. Squeezing my eyes shut does no good, the memories just come faster. However, when I open my eyes, they are only met with darkness. My mind is lost, my soul in turmoil. I can't find the way out. I try every breathing exercise I read about after leaving Kurt. Nothing is working.

I don't know how long I've been standing here, but when there is a knock on the back door I scream. Startled and scared. Slowly, and on wobbly legs, I make my way to the door. "Capri? Are you there?" I hear Jayse call out. His deep voice muffled from the metal door standing between us. Yanking it open I feel the burst of ice-cold air rushing in. Jayse stands there looking like my hero. Without thinking, I rush into his arms. His body is warm compared to the air moving around us. A strangled sob breaks free from my chest. I have no idea where it comes from, but Jayse just pulls me tighter against him. One hand gently rubs circles on my back and the other is wrapped around the back of my neck, securing me. At this moment, I feel protected and that's something I've never felt before. "It's okay, Bright Eyes, I'm here."

Sometime later the tears stop, the anxiety subsides, and I step away from Jayse's embrace. Completely embarrassed I start to move around the kitchen cleaning up the rest of the stuff I haven't gotten to yet. Jayse stands in the doorway. I don't look at him, but I can feel his eyes on me. "Talk to me."

I shake my head. "There's nothing to say."

"I'm going to call that a lie right now. There's definitely something to say."

Anger burns in my belly. I have no good reason to be angry at Jayse but he's the only one here and anger is rarely rational. "Really? If you have so much to say, then why don't you talk?"

He steps inside, his large size eating up a good portion of the distance I had put between us. The heavy metal door slams shut. I nearly jump out of my skin as it rings out in the dark and silence. "I know you deserve the answers to every question you have, but I'm not ready."

"Maybe I wasn't either."

Jayse pinches the bridge of his nose. "I didn't ask you to share anything with me. You volunteered that information, and yes, I'm beyond thankful for the strength you showed by doing that, but I'm not there yet."

I laugh, but it's harsh and there is no real amusement in the sound. "Strength? I don't have strength, Jayse. I run whenever things get too hard. I live my life looking over my shoulder constantly wondering if Kurt has caught up to me yet. I'm a freaking mess!" I throw my hands up in frustration. "Every day I wake up wondering if it's all going to come crashing down. Kurt told me I was his, he owned me, and I'd never be free. I believed him. I still do. Eventually, my past life will catch up with me. I can't run from the devil forever."

Spinning away from him, I busy myself with organizing the already clean canister set on the counter. "You thought he had found you tonight." Jayse doesn't ask, he simply states. "That's why you were so emotional when you opened the door." The moment he starts to move towards me I back away. "Capri, I'm not him. I get that he wasn't a good guy but no matter what I'll do what I can to protect you. He won't get to you if he ever finds you." His hands wrap around my upper arms and pull me into his chest. I want to fight it, but I'm utterly exhausted. For a long time, we stand there like this. Jayse holding me. I breathe in the scent of mint and wood, all things that will forever remind me of Jayse. I'm supposed to be learning from my mistakes but instead I'm falling for yet another man. While I don't think he will ever lay a hand on me the way Kurt or Eddie did, I do believe he will be the one to destroy my heart without ever meaning to.

TWELVE

Jayse

After we finished cleaning Bee's Batter, I took out the trash as Capri locked the back door. She had been so shaken up by the power being out. I hadn't expected to find her in such distress. When she started crying, it broke my heart. I wanted to take all her fear away from her. Then she became defensive. I know she wants answers, and she deserves them, but I'm just not ready to give them yet. I wish I was. She has been the first person I've wanted to open up to since that tragic night, but I just don't know how yet. When she started to lash out at me, I understood it was just a defense mechanism, but it was difficult to take for a moment.

Once she's safely tucked away in her car, I pull around her and lead us out of the alley and back through town to her apartment. Every few seconds I glance at my rearview mirror to make sure she is still there, following me through the darkened streets of

Blue Ridge. Cops are parked at all the major intersections in town to direct any traffic that might be out, but for the most part the roads are empty. We passed one car the entire drive. Finally, we pulled up to Carpi's apartment. I park behind her and make my way towards her. It's an eerie feeling with complete darkness around us. "Do you want to come to my house?" The invitation is out of my mouth before I can even think about it. The entire drive I knew I had wanted to stay with her, wanted to protect her and calm the anxiety that had left her body rigid. I knew I'd never invite myself in and there was a good chance she wouldn't extend an invitation. Clearly, she was a little frustrated with me, understandably so.

With the darkness I can't see her face clearly, but I can feel the shock of my invitation coming off her in waves. "What?"

Suddenly, my mouth felt like cotton. My tongue seemed welded to the roof of my mouth. Nerves set off in my body like fireworks on the fourth of July. "Hmm... I was wondering if you wanted to come to my house. I mean with the electricity and everything off it might be nice to not be alone. Plus, I have a generator that I can start up if it stays off too long."

"Are you sure?" she asks.

There's a good chance that she's noticed a certain pattern I have. If she's paid attention over the period of time we have lived across from one another then she more than likely knows that no one comes into my house except my parents, sister and Everett. That house has been a safe haven since I purchased it and started to fix it up. It was something that helped me through my darkest days shortly after the accident happened. My house is the one place I always feel like I don't have to put on a show for everyone else, I don't have to hide. "Yes, I'm sure." My voice sounds more assured than I feel. I hold my breath while I wait for her answer.

"Okay." It's a simple answer. One word. However, it makes me both excited and nervous. The idea of having Capri inside the walls of my safe haven is hard to explain. Excitement over it is the pure fact that I enjoy being around her. Everything about her brings a calm over me, silences my demons that can be so loud. She is something completely unique. I'm nervous because there's a good chance this could make or break whatever is going on between us. I didn't plan on having her over so evidence of my former life could possibly, and probably will, be seen. I'll have no choice but to explain, but then again maybe that's why I invited her. A part of me is terrified that I'll never explain my history to her because I'm a coward. She thinks I'm a hero of some sort, but in reality, I'm a terrified little boy. If something doesn't intervene to make me explain everything to her, I might never face it. Sure, she could ask around and find out about me, but I'd rather she hears my side of the story.

Without another thought, I hit the button to lock my truck and take her hand in mine. I lead us across the alley and through the backyard, up to my back door. I push it open and lead us inside. Releasing her hand, I make my way to the kitchen counter where I left the candles sitting and light them once more. "Do you not lock your door?" Capri asks.

I shake my head. "Not my back door."

"That doesn't worry you?"

I pass one of the candles to her and she takes it as I lead us to the living room. We take a seat on the couch on opposite ends. She kicks her Converse off and pulls her legs under her. "I grew up here. Blue Ridge has very little crime. Besides, if someone is that desperate then they must really need whatever they're after."

"What if you walk in on someone while trying to rob your house? They could kill you!" Her seafoam green eyes are bugged out as she stares at me. The candlelight has given her a golden glow and it does something to my heart.

My shoulders shrug. "That's the least of my worries." Capri shakes her head. "I was never one to be afraid of death. I think to a certain extent you have to come to peace with that before you sign up to be a firefighter. It's your job to run into open flames and unknown situations. When everyone else is running away from the flames, you have to run into them. You have to depend on man-made equipment and suits and all you have to survive is the grace of God. You have to make yourself okay with the possibility of dying every single day."

Silence falls upon us. She stares at me, studying me in a way that is kind of uncomfortable. "You seem to have really loved it. Why did you quit?"

At that exact moment, the lights come back on. Saved by the lights, you could say. I smile at her. "Looks like the lights are back."

A sadness crosses her face. "So, it seems."

"Don't get too excited," I tease her, as I nudge her knee with one of my feet.

"I kind of liked the dark once I got used to it."

My eyebrows pull together in confusion. There's no way she liked the dark. It sent her into a downward spiral earlier. "Are you sure about that?"

"Yeah, you seemed more open in the dark."

Her words sink into my skin and pour into my soul. I stand up and head to the kitchen. Rummaging through the cabinets, all I can find is some boxed instant rice and canned Chinese Chicken Chow Mein. "Are you hungry?" I ask her.

She laughs. "I used to love this stuff!"

"Good, since it's all I have. I don't cook much. Most of the time I just grab something from one of the food places in town."

"That makes sense," she says. "If you give me the pans, I'll cook it."

As I grab the pans, I pass them to her, but I'm still going to help. "You asked why I quit." She stops opening the can and stares at me. I don't meet her eyes, but I can feel them on me. "I went into being a firefighter right after high school. I was pretty naive to be honest. I thought I could save everyone. Maybe, that's a common thing for firefighters. I don't know, but then something happened, and it made me realize I can't save everyone, especially, if I can't even save myself."

"Jayse, I don't believe that."

I turn back to look at her now. I'm unable to ignore that invisible pull to her. "It's because you see me one way. I am the person you see me as sometimes, but it's not all there is to me."

Capri steps forward. She stands toe-to-toe with me and her big green eyes look up at me. "I know there is more to you, but I don't think that any of that would make me see you differently. I've watched you these past few years and I think I know you better than you think I do. Besides, we all have a past. We've all made decisions we aren't necessarily proud of, but I'll never judge a person based on that alone. There is more to a person than those few moments of weakness or failure."

My chest tightens. Lungs constrict. Emotion mixes with the blood in my veins confusing my head. I sway slightly on my feet almost as if the world has just tilted. Maybe it has. Everything with Capri is different so maybe she did tilt my world. Slowly, she raises a hand to rest on my cheek. Her eyes are open and honest. "I don't know where you came from," I admit quietly.

She gives me a teasing smile. "From all over really."

I lean forehead against hers. "Very funny."

Capri shrugs her shoulders. "I thought so."

"I'm pretty damn sure I don't deserve you or an ounce of your understanding, but I'm a weak man when it comes to you and I'm going to take it."

The quick intake of breath doesn't go unnoticed by me. I caught her off guard. "Good, I want you to." Her voice is slightly breathless when she replies. Her green eyes light up with something I haven't seen in a long time. My lips find hers as we devour one another as if it's our last day on Earth and this is our dying wish.

THIRTEEN

Capri

I wake up to the smell of canned Chicken Chow Mein. My stomach grumbles like I didn't feed it yesterday, which I did, more than normal. As I roll over, I find the other spot of the bed is cold. Jayse has been out of it longer than just to cook the food we had forgotten about last night. Sitting up I take in his room. Surprisingly, it's clean and neat. I'm used to the type of guys who throw everything on the floor and never clean anything, then again Jayse doesn't have someone to go around and pick up after him. I pull the sheet tighter around my body. Last night had been...amazing but now I'm wondering how big of a mistake I just made. He won't tell me about his past, he's still so guarded and I made a promise to myself that I obviously just broke. Did I just make a huge mistake?

My head and heart are at war once again. My heart, the traitor that it is, believes I made the right decision. It's possible that it's correct. Jayse has changed a good bit in the past few days. I've been going through what memories I have of him since I moved to Blue Ridge and in every one, he's sullen and broody, never smiling, guarded and withdrawn from those around him. I still wish he'd open up to me more, but my heart believes he will after we spend more time with one another. I do know that he's never had a woman spend the night with him. He's home every night. Do I think he's perfect? No, I'm sure he's not, but I don't think he's a bad guy either.

My head on the other hand is telling me how foolish I am. I let my guard down with yet another man. Regret and disappointment is already settling in my gut. No matter how I try to push it away it doesn't leave. I betrayed myself and the promise I made to myself years ago. Was it a mistake? It could have been, but I really hope it wasn't. Jayse, seems more sincere than any other guy I've met, but then Kurt comes to mind. I can still picture him so vividly. He had seemed to be kind, patient, understanding and as if he truly loved me. Come to find out he was none of those things. He was cruel, vengeful, controlling and he didn't love me at all.

Jayse appears in the doorway. A pair of navy-blue basketball shorts hanging low on his hips. Shirtless the scars that cover at least half of his right-side torso and all of his right arm and shoulder are visible. The moonlight coming in from the blinds seems to illuminate that marred skin. He leans one arm against the frame of the doorway. "Oh good, you're awake."

I try to smile, but I know it's failing miserably. "Yeah, I am."

"Are you alright?" he asks, concern is easily heard in his voice.

"Yeah, I'm fine," I lie through my teeth, as my stomach churns and rolls with nausea. Once again, I try to smile at him. His eyebrows knit together in confusion.

He definitely doesn't believe me as he nods his head. He's going to accept what I'm saying but his body language tells me everything I need to know. "Well, I woke up and I was starving so I made us the canned Chicken Chow Mein." I watch as he walks over to the dresser directly across from the bed. He opens a drawer, pulls something out and turns back around to face me. A shirt lands at my feet. "There's something clean you can wear if you don't want to get completely dressed."

I don't get to say thank you before he leaves the room. I pull on the oversized t-shirt and make my way to the kitchen. My stomach grumbles as if it hasn't had food in days. "That smells really good."

"Thanks," he says, glancing over his shoulder. He stops stirring the pan in front of him and releases a low whistle of appreciation. "Well, if I knew you were going to make my shirt look that good, I might have tried to get you into one sooner."

The blush heats my cheeks as I shake my head. "You're being silly."

Jayse places a plate in front of me. "I'm being honest." He leans down and lightly brushes his lips against mine. I can either sink or swim. It's now or never. A decision needs to be made. If I sink, I sink into him and whatever this is between us. If I swim, I'm running again. Not looking back at what's left behind, only moving forward. One of his hands tangles in my hair and I sink. I sink so fast I feel like an anchor in a bottomless ocean. When he pulls away his smile is so large that his gray eyes crinkle in the corners. "I'll never get enough of that." He kisses the tip of my nose and moves away, making his own plate of food before sitting across from me. After a few bites, he looks up at me with curious eyes. "Are you okay?"

My head bobs up and down. "Yeah, of course, why?"

He lays his fork next to his plate and studies me. "You've been acting... different ever since I came into the room, and you were awake."

"I haven't," I reply, too quickly, too defensively.

I watch as his eyebrows arch up. "You have. Do you mind letting me in on what's going on?"

A heavy sigh escaped me. "I just broke a promise."

"To whom?" he asks.

My eyes move to scan the dining room and kitchen area. "To myself," I finally admit.

"Okay, Bright Eyes. I'm still not following. I need more of an explanation."

The fire of unreasonable anger burns in my belly. I'm not actually mad at Jayse, but I'm about to take my personal anger out on him. It's completely unfair, but the words are on the tip of my tongue. "I made a promise to myself to never make these kinds of mistakes again."

For a moment, Jayse looks genuinely confused then I think the meaning of my words sink in. "These kinds of mistakes?"

I roll my eyes. I guess I've decided to swim after all. "Yes, Jayse. I told you about my history. I don't want to keep repeating it yet here I am."

"I'm not like your exes," he says, through clenched teeth.

The worst part about this is that I know he's nothing like any of them. Jayse is in a league of his own. Whoever created him smashed the mold afterwards. He is truly one of a kind. I can tell that within just the amount of time I've spent with him. It hasn't been much time, but it's been more than enough. "So, you say. They've all said something similar though."

Silence falls between us. We stare at each other, each one silently begging the other to reach forward and close the growing distance but neither of us will. Both of us are too damaged to do that. "If that's how you feel then maybe you're right. This was a mistake."

His words slice at me as I'm sure mine just did to him. I stand up silently and make my way to the bedroom. I dress quickly and then make my way back through the house to the back door. My hand rests on the doorknob for a moment, but he doesn't say anything, so I yank it open and make my way back to my apartment. My heart is resting at the bottom of the ocean, sad and broken. My head is yelling victory for walking away. Both are being dramatic.

When I reach my apartment, I shut the door and my back slides down until I hit the floor. Tears leak down my face. Thora watches me from across the room. Eventually, she makes her way over to me, but she's just another reminder of him now.

FOURTEEN

Jayse

It's been a week. A week since Capri's guards came up and locked me out of her life. A week since I let her walk away without even trying to fight for her. I know that if I had tried that more than likely it would have been wasted time, but a part of me wonders if that's not what she needs. Someone to fight for her. Someone to show her that she is worth every obstacle you might have to face. Someone to show her that she is indeed worth everything. I have this sinking feeling in my gut that she's never had that before.

Capri smiles and flirts. Confidence in every action shines through but I wonder if it's more of a show. Is she as confident as she seems? For some reason, as I lie in bed at night watching the ceiling fan above me make slow rotations, I question this. Nightmares aren't currently haunting me, but then again, I'm not really sleeping. I keep trying to figure out where everything went wrong. Capri wants to keep the world at arm's length, to never get hurt again. I don't blame her for that, but the problem is that it isn't a practical plan. You'll never be able to keep everyone far enough away to avoid being hurt. I know firsthand that doesn't work. I've tried it for years and foolishly I thought I was succeeding, but then Capri showed up in my life. I got too close to her and now I'm consumed.

This week is the last week of Bushels of Fun. The local fall festival that is held every year. After this, you'll still be able to pick pumpkins and apples, but the rest of the activities will be gone until next year. Blue Ridge can be magical during this time of year if you allow it. All of the leaves changing colors, the cooler breeze coming off the mountains, the fresh scent in the air. Everyone seems to be energized in a different way. Maybe, it's the change of temperatures. Whatever causes it the whole town joins in for the fall festival.

****

I've been working all day on rebuilding this porch. For a moment, I stop to wipe the sweat from my face when I hear the crunch of tires on the gravel circle driveway behind me. When I turn around, I see Everett. He climbs out of his charcoal gray Ford truck and heads my way. "Howdy," I greet him.

Everett laughs and shakes his head. "You always throw me off when you greet me that way."

"You should be used to it. I've done it since we were in school," I remind him. He extends an ice-cold bottle of water to me. I gladly take it. Bringing the cold liquid to my lips I chug half the bottle.

"Word to the wise, you might want to take a break every now and then to hydrate. Your sister is a nurse, right?" he asks.

Rolling my eyes and turning back around, I start working on the porch once more. "You know that she is. I mean, you were a lovesick puppy over her for years so I'm pretty sure you know more about her than I do sometimes." Silence falls between us. The tension, that suddenly fills the space between Everett and I, shocks me. I stand up and turn back around to look at him. Everett looks like a deer frozen in headlights. "What's wrong?"

I watch as his Adam's apple bobs as he swallows. He looks terrified and I'm not entirely sure why. "So, I needed to talk to you about something."

This must be serious if he looks like this. Everett is clearly nervous, so I place the hammer in my hand back into the tool belt hanging on my waist. As I approach, Everett his eyes seem to widen even more. "What's up man?"

"So, you know how you said I was always a lovesick puppy over Whitney?"

I chuckle and nod my head. "Yeah, it was obvious, man." I'm laughing as I think back to our high school days, but then the dots start to connect in my head. My laughter dies out and I realize the reason he is so nervous is because whatever he needs to tell me, has to do with my little sister. Somehow, I have an idea about what he needs to tell me. "I'm guessing it has to do with Whitney."

Everett's eyebrows shoot up in surprise. "We've been talking."

"Since when? How?" I ask.

"A few weeks." He shrugs his shoulders. "She came into the store after her shift looking for some stuff to fix a leaking sink. I helped her out, but the next day she came by again and said it didn't work. For some reason, she didn't seem to want to bother you, so I volunteered to go by and check it out for her. I got it fixed and she insisted on fixing me dinner as a thank you. Cayley was with the babysitter so I told her I couldn't but then she told me to bring her as well. Cayley loved Whitney and vice versa. Whitney was great with her. Afterwards, we just hung out and talked for a really long time. We exchanged numbers and we've been texting ever since and I asked her to the autumn ball dance at the end of the week, but then I got worried because I really should have asked you if it was okay first."

I hold up my dirty hands to stop him from talking anymore. Everett's mouth slams shut, and I can see the worry in his eyes. I smile at him, and I watch as his shoulders relax some. "I'm not upset, Everett. I'm actually really happy for y'all. There's only one thing I need to say...don't hurt my baby sister. I don't think that you would because you've basically been in love with her for the majority of your life, but it's my brotherly duty to threaten you. Don't make me have to kick your ass."

Everett sighs. "I didn't sleep at all last night worrying about asking you."

"You never needed to ask me. Whitney is a grown woman who can't be told what to do, not that I would even try," I tell him with a chuckle.

Everett bobs his head. "You are right about that."

"I actually wish you luck. Between Cayley and Whitney, you are going to have your hands full." I clap him on the back a few times.

"I'll take it," he tells me, with a mushy smile. I wonder if I smiled like this at anyone while I was thinking about Capri. I know it's possible, but I really hope I didn't. "So, what about you?" Everett asks, as I head back towards the porch to finish it up. I stop and turn back around to face him.

"What about me?"

He raises his eyebrows. "You and Capri Owens."

Immediately, my fingers move up to pinch the bridge of my nose. "There is no me and Capri Owens, so I have no idea what you're talking about."

"Say whatever you want, but there was something. You two were spotted all over town together. Normally, I'd say no big deal, but this is you we're talking about, Jayse. That is a big deal, a really big deal. Everyone noticed and talked about it."

"Everyone should mind their own damn business. What I do or don't do shouldn't be town gossip." Frustration and anger courses through my body like a racing car pumping gas.

"Jayse, you know how Blue Ridge works. It's a small town and it thrives on gossip. It's how it goes. You're the town's golden boy. Won a state championship. All around good guy. The town adores you, Jayse."

I shake my head so hard some of my hair escapes the hair tie holding my hair in a low ponytail. Rejecting his words. Once upon a time, I was the guy he just described, but I haven't been in a long time. "I'm not him anymore."

"The hell you aren't! This porch that you're fixing for Mr. Cower, is he paying you for the work?" Silence falls between us. "I know for a fact that he doesn't have the income to pay for the repair, but this old porch was dangerous. You're still the same guy."

"The hell I am!" My voice rises in anger.

Everett slams a hand down on the wooden post I'm using to make the porch fence. "Yes, you are. You might have closed the world off from yourself, but the world didn't turn its back on you. Just because you couldn't save Bradee and Sam and that doesn't mean the town turned its back on you. You've created your own personal hell that you just live in constantly. Capri was the first person who managed to get in, past all the broody bullshit you throw at people. You deserve to be happy again. Bradee would have wanted that, you know she would have. So be happy, Jayse." He turns around and leaves. I don't turn around until I'm certain he's out of the driveway and heading down the street. His words run round and round in my head. I finish up the porch then head home to shower. As I stand in my bathroom, I know what I have to do from here.

FIFTEEN

Capri

It's amazing how someone can become such a huge part of your life in such a short amount of time. Jayse and I had no more than a week's worth of actual time combined that we spent together, yet since I walked out of his house last week it feels like years. My mind often wanders to him and what he is doing. What project is he working on? I've closed my curtains that cover the windows facing the alley and Jayse's backyard. I can't bring myself to look at him. I've managed to keep my eyes averted every time I leave my apartment from looking in his direction. My heart aches, which sounds dumb and naive.

When I walked away that night my head and heart felt like they were locked in an internal war. Neither could agree on anything and I was at a loss of what to do. I wanted to follow my heart, but I had done that so often and it had gotten me nowhere. Convinced that things with Jayse would be the same I ended up listening to my head, but now it seems like it might have switched sides as well. Now, it's my head and heart at war with my pride. I'm too prideful to walk across that alley and ask him how he is.

As I head down the stairs, I eye the covered canvas and easel in the corner. The two curtains on the outer windows are drawn shut, only allowing the light from the middle window to fill the living room. I haven't touched that canvas since I came in that night. I had looked at it through my tear-filled eyes, the image I had painted blurry but perfectly clear in my head. Taking a sheet from the corner I had tossed it over the easel, trying to silence my emotions. It was a picture of him. It was him...at least in my mind. Looking at it was just too much to bear. After I covered the canvas, I pulled the curtains. They had come with the apartment when I moved in, but I had always opted to leave them open. I loved the way the natural light filtered inside, and it made my painting corner perfect, but now I can't even find it in me to even try.

Thora was lounging on the windowsill of the middle window. Her head popped up to watch me as I made my way to the kitchen where I started a cup of coffee before grabbing my basket of laundry sitting next to the door and heading downstairs. The moment I stepped inside the laundry room, I felt him. His presence was still here lingering in the small room. The memories of him fixing the washer rushes back to me. I really am being ridiculous; I mumble to myself.

Once I have the laundry washing, I go back upstairs and fix my coffee before sitting in front of the TV. Zoning out on mindless television seems like a good idea. For a couple of hours, I sit on the couch, coffee mug in hand, the hot coffee long since gone cold until I realize it's time for my shift at Bee's Batter. I dress quickly and warmly since the chill in the air has turned cold overnight.

Fleece lined black leggings, a long purple tunic, and black leather jacket paired with over the knee boots feels warm enough to me. I throw my hair into a messy bun, slip on my purple framed glasses and grab my black, fluffy earmuffs and gloves before heading down to my car. Giving my car some time to warm up is hard because as soon as I slide into the driver's seat I want to get as far away from his backyard as possible. It's almost as if I can hear it calling to me, begging me to just look in its direction, but I don't. Instead, I turn up the music and drown out my thoughts. Two songs later I'm heading to work.

There are no parking spaces along the front of Bee's Batter. With the colder temperature and this being the last week of Bushels of Fun, I'm not shocked, so I circle around back, using the alley and park behind Warbee and Jolie's vehicles. The back door is locked so I knock and wait. Teaganne, Warbee's best friend, opens the door. Her long, sleek raven colored hair is down and flowing around her hips. She smiles. "Oh, come inside, it's freezing out there." She moves aside to let me into the kitchen. The warmth hits me instantly followed by all those smells that I love so much, pumpkin, apple, brown sugar, cinnamon, nutmeg. My stomach growls. "I almost didn't recognize you with the hair color change."

I smile. Teaganne is gorgeous. She's a fashion designer turned interior designer but really, she should be a model. She's tall and curvy with flawless olive skin. Her honey eyes are bright and kind with a hint of intelligence and determination. Teaganne has long raven hair that hangs around her waist. She reminds me of Cleopatra, which makes sense since she's half Egyptian. "Yeah, I felt like maybe I should start to tone it down for a little bit. I've gotten lucky and it hasn't done as much damage as I thought it would."

"That's always great, but don't tell Seraphina or she'll start to think you aren't a mermaid." Teaganne winks and laughs. Seraphina is Teaganne's little girl who is just a toddler. From the moment she saw me, she believed I was a mermaid. My ever-changing hair color made her believe I was one of the underwater creatures.

I smile back. "I'll keep the secret." I can hear chatter, music, and commotion coming from beyond the kitchen doors that lead into the main area of the bakery. I point towards them. "Are we busy today?"

Teaganne bobs her head up and down with wide eyes. "So busy! Warbee and I had a meeting with a possible client earlier and when I dropped her back off the place was swamped, so I offered to help for a bit. I'm just pulling things out and putting new stuff in when the timers go off. "

"Wow, she could have called me in earlier," I comment.

"I don't think she wanted to bother you. Honestly, we figured it'd die down after lunch, but it hasn't yet. I'm so glad to see you now though." One of the many timers starts beeping so Teaganne gets busy with switching the baking sheets out. I rush towards the back where we keep our personal belongings. I grab my apron and tie it around my waist as I head back through the bakery and out to the front.

Jolie sighs in relief at the sight of me. Warbee smiles. "I'm so glad you're here."

"You should have called me earlier. I would have come in," I tell her. Stepping up beside her I help her fill the boxes lining the back counter with the orders sitting in front of them.

"I know you would have but you also need some time off." Warbee moves over to the coffee maker and starts filling to go cups.

Once my boxes are full, I take the boxes to the side counter where some people are waiting and start to distribute stuff out. Warbee appears with two drink holders full of drinks. "What happened?" I ask.

She stops to wipe her forehead with the back of her hand. Her glasses slip down her nose and she pushes them back up. "I'm not sure. Bushels of Fun is packed. My mom called and gave me a head's up that they were almost out of food, so I instantly started baking up new batches, but then it got crazy in here. Thankfully, Teaganne was here and could pull the baking sheets in and out."

Jolie slides some more orders our way. Warbee and I get to work on boxes, bags, and to go cups. Jocelynn, one of the local newspaper reporters, steps up. "Did y'all hear?"

I look at the leggy, blonde with hair as big as Texas itself. Her perfectly straight, overly whitened teeth bites down into her collagen filled bottom lip. "The Sip and Smack is closed until further notice."

Warbee's head whips in Jocelyn's direction. Things between the Sip and Smack and Bee's Batter were slightly heated a couple of months ago. Sip and Smack was a new restaurant and while Warbee was in full support of a new business for the residents of Blue Ridge, Fran, the owner of Sip and Smack, was a real piece of work. She believed she was special apparently. Every time she was around, she made people feel small and then she hired a bakery chef to add to her menu. Totally unfair considering that Warbee is the best baker in town, but the newness of the business took from ours. Teaganne and her boyfriend, Keefer, who also happens to be one of Warbee's best friends, revamped the bakery and website and now things are booming, but I'd be lying if I said I wasn't curious about what happened at the Sip and Smack. Most of the time, I try to keep my ears out of the local gossip mill, but this one feels almost necessary. Warbee comes over, forgetting the order she was working on. "What happened?" she asks.

"Well, from what I heard there was a possible gas leak in the building so the gas has been turned off and everything has to be fixed before Fran can reopen." Jocelyn wags her eyebrows like this is the juiciest bit of gossip she's ever heard. I doubt it is considering she's a reporter for a living.

Warbee places her hand over her heart. "Oh goodness." That's the thing about Warbee; she has the heart of a saint. No matter what you do to her she still feels for you if something goes wrong. Don't mistake that though as her being a pushover because she's definitely not a pushover.

"That's what I said when I got the post-it passed to me. I'm actually heading over to try and get a comment or interview with Fran to see what she has to say about all of it."

I clear my throat. "Is that even possible, though? Didn't she have to have an inspection on the building when she bought it and if something was wrong, wouldn't she know about it?"

Jocelyn's smile is wicked when it appears on her face. "That's the thing she would have. I'm thinking she probably should have had it fixed but didn't and look where it got her. Serves her right for trying to take out the bakery if you ask me. Well, I'm off to get the scoop. Y'all better get prepared for one busy day and possibly many more to come." Jocelyn waved as she heads out of the bakery. Warbee and I exchange a look, before she goes back to the box, she was filling with her homemade autumn inspired donuts.

After I catch up on the drinks and start brewing fresh pots of coffee and tea, I move towards Warbee and start helping fill the orders. "You should go start baking some more stuff up."

"We're swamped. I can't leave y'all." She glances at me quickly and I can read the indecision in her eyes.

I nudge her shoulders. "Go. We're swamped, but if we run out of food it'll be worse. Go bake. Send Teaganne to help me."

"Are you sure?" she asks. I can tell she's worried and probably feeling a little guilty, but she shouldn't. Any of us can take or fill the orders, but none of us can bake like her so I nod my head. She rushes to the kitchen and a few minutes later Teaganne appears with an apron around her waist. It's actually funny looking considering her sky-high heeled boots and long sleeve sweater dress. Her hair is pulled up into a ponytail and she smiles as she joins me.

For the next few hours, it's nonstop. Teaganne, Jolie, and I take more orders than I could have ever imagined. Warbee had to stop and place an order with our vendor for more coffee, tea, and products she uses to bake. By the time it slows down, we all look like a semi-truck has run us over. Since I came in later, I send everyone else home and promise to call them if it gets swamped again, but by the look in the sky a storm is brewing. Most people will be tucked home at this point or enjoying the last few nights of Bushels of Fun, but the drop in temperature has me doubting that it's packed tonight.

I'm just about to head to the door to lock up when the bell above chimes. I turn around but the greeting dies on my tongue. Jayse is standing there, taking up so much space that he almost looks larger than life. His stormy gray eyes meet mine and they remind me of the storm brewing outside the walls of the bakery. Jayse has a storm brewing within his walls, too, and I'm not sure I'm strong enough to weather it. "Looks like you had a busy day."

His jeans are just loose enough to make my heart patter and the black t-shirt he has on hugs his body. A red and black flannel over that and a denim jacket makes him look like a true Georgia boy. He runs a hand through his hair which is down and loose. It's my favorite look on him even though he doesn't wear it like this often. "Yeah, you could say that." We stand there awkwardly and in silence. Finally, I ask, "Did you need coffee or something to eat?"

I start to move towards the counter when he replies. "No."

Okay...I think to myself. I turn back around to face him. "Then what are you doing here?"

"I need you, Capri. I need to talk to you."

My heart stops because for a foolish moment I think he might tell me his story. I think he might open up to me, but almost as quickly as that thought enters my head it disappears. It's wishful thinking. I have walls, but Jayse has walls wrapped in electrical barb wire. No one is getting through, and he isn't about to open that gate. "I don't think there's anything to say."

"There's plenty left to say. Are you closing up?" he asks. I nod my head. "After you're done, will you go with me?"

My eyebrows pull together. "Go where?"

"To the cemetery." His eyes refuse to meet mind. The way his body is angled, feels like he's struggling. I want to go to him, but it won't end well for either of us, so I just plant my feet to the floor.

"You do realize how strange that request sounds, right?"

Jayse nods his head. "Yeah, but it's the only place that feels right."

I nibble on my bottom lip. Why am I even considering this? Because you're a dumb girl who just wants to be near him. I knew I missed him but being back in his presence is overwhelming. "I don't know…"

"Please," he says. His voice and eyes are pleading, and they pull at that invisible string between us. My heart and head both screams yes so, I nod my head. "Thank you," he says quietly. "Do you want some help closing up?"

As tired as I am, I know I can't let him stay. Being around him is difficult and since I've agreed to go to a cemetery with him once I'm done, I think I need some time to prepare myself. In his absence, I realized how much he means to me and now I can't ignore it. "No, thank you, I'm good. It should only take about forty-five minutes."

He seems to understand that I need time to myself. "Okay, I'll meet you there." Without another word, he turns around and leaves. I watch until he's no longer visible and the roar of his motorcycle is nothing but a distant memory.

I had a plan to keep my distance, but like all my plans...it fell through the cracks. At this point, I don't even know what I'm doing or what promises I'm breaking. I just know that the biggest part of me wants to be near Jayse. I want to be the one to comfort him because right now I feel like that's what he needs most. New energy courses through my veins and I rush around cleaning everything up. Forty-three minutes later, I step out of the back door of the bakery and into my car. I send a quick text to let him know I'm on my way.

SIXTEEN

Jayse

The wind makes its way through my denim jacket, freezing me to my core. Memories come to mind, but I push them away, now isn't the time or place to take a ride down memory lane. I need to save it until Capri meets me. As I make my way to the cemetery, I drive past Bushels of Fun. It's not as busy as it has been. I think the sudden drop in temperature may have something to do with it.

The black intricately designed iron gates of the cemetery are closed. I park the bike and climb off before heading in the direction of the gates. Right after the fire, I'd come here so often, looking back I feel almost pathetic. I'd scale the cement brick wall that doubled a fence most nights. I'm actually surprised as I look back that I didn't break any bones. Anyways, one night Isaac, the grounds keeper, found me trying to climb my way over the wall. He helped me down and showed me the trick to opening the gates. When I asked him why he got a faraway look in his eye. "I've lost someone, too. I know what you're looking for. You won't find it here, but that's something you'll have to realize on your own. In the meantime, I'd rather see you on this side of the dirt." After that, he had turned around and walked away.

Learning the trick to the gate was perfect. It definitely made coming into the cemetery easier. However, after meeting Isaac his words constantly stayed with me. Every night, under the moonlight I would sneak in here, but I didn't feel so alone anymore. His words seeped further and further into my soul until I finally realized they were true. With that realization, I started to come to the cemetery less and less. Things within me slowly started to heal some. I knew the guilt, regret, and hurt would never fully go away, not that I even wanted it to. The way I saw it, I had failed, and I deserved the weight of what I felt.

With the gate left open for Capri, I climb back onto the bike and drive towards the headstone I know like the back of my hand. The one that haunts my every thought. When I come to a stop, I take a moment to take a deep breath and collect myself. The pricking at the back of my eyes causes me to squeeze them shut, fighting off the tears I can feel coming. I sit on the back of the bike while I wait for Capri to arrive. About half an hour later headlights flooded the darkened area. As I turn around, I see Capri's Chevy Sonic slowly making its way down through the cemetery. I climb off the back of my bike as she comes to a stop. She looks uncertain as she climbs out of the car. Her seafoam green eyes scan the area around us. "This place is closed. Should we be here?" she whispers.

"Why are you whispering?" I ask.

She looks around again before shrugging her shoulders. "It seems like a place you should. You know, rest in peace, and all that. It's so quiet that it's either borderline peaceful or eerie, depending on how you look at it. You still didn't answer my question."

"Well, the answer to your question is part of this long story, but to give a brief answer the cemetery is closed but I know the grounds keeper so it's okay to be here." I start to move down the row of headstones. Moving on autopilot. I come to a stop and Capri stops a few steps behind me. I know the moment she notices the headstone in front of us, because she intakes a sharp breath. The recognition hits her and me. I wasn't expecting to feel the flood of emotions by bringing Capri here. Bradee and Samuel Lyon are engraved into the stone. My heart sinks every time I read their names permanently etched into the stone, but forever gone from this world.

"I don't understand…" Capri says quietly.

I sigh before diving into the story that made me who I am today. "Bradee and I grew up on the same street. She was my best friend. Everywhere one of us went the other was never far behind. When we got to school, we had all the same classes. It was that typical story of best friends falling in love and living happily ever after.

Except we didn't. I don't know how much you know about my past and football career, but before Rocker Gordon made this town proud, it was supposed to be me. I had a full ride scholarship to a college of my choice to play football. I'd be on the fast track to the NFL in no time, but then Bradee got sick. It turns out that Bradee wasn't sick, but she was pregnant. That changed everything. I know a lot of people probably thought I was just doing what was right by Bradee, but I loved her, and I loved the idea of being a father. It didn't bother me at all to leave football behind. Instead of going off to college we graduated high school, got married, I became a firefighter, and we had Sam. He was the perfect little boy with his mom's red hair and freckles and my gray eyes." I have to stop as emotion crawls up my throat, making it difficult to breathe or talk. Capri steps closer to me and wraps a hand around my elbow, rubbing her thumb slowly up and down the inside. It's soothing. "We had just bought a cute one story, three-bedroom house. We just barely got moved in before Halloween. We were excited to spend the holidays in the house we planned to call home for many years. It was early December, a big snowstorm rolled in and the temperatures dropped well below freezing. I was at the station when the call came through. The minute I heard the address through the scanner, my heart stopped. Nothing in my body worked properly. It felt like I was standing outside in the middle of the snowstorm without anything on to protect my body. To this day, I don't know how I managed to get onto the truck. The storm had made getting to our house on the outskirts of town incredibly hard and time-consuming. By the time we made it to the outskirts of town where the house was, the smoke clouded the air, and the flames were dancing in the night sky. We all knew from the call that Bradee and Sam were trapped. The rest of the team tried to get me to stay, but I rushed forward and into the house. Everything I had ever learned; all my training went right out the window. The only thing that mattered was getting to them. I did freeze though. When I first walked inside, I froze. I had been in fires before, but it was nothing like seeing the inside of your home being eaten up by flames. All the memories, all of our belongings...just gone."

Capri tenses beside me and I know she can probably guess how this is probably going to end. My voice has become thick with emotion. "I'll always wonder if that pause is what caused them to die. I moved forward and every door was open except the master bedroom. As I reached for the door, the roof came down. I don't remember much after that except waking up in the hospital and being told I had third degree burns on a third of my body. I didn't care about myself. My only thought was Bradee and Sam. When I asked and everyone looked uncomfortable, I knew but I needed to hear it. Finally, my dad stepped forward and explained that when the roof collapsed, they had become trapped under the burning wood, and they passed away before anyone was able to reach them."

Tears are steaming silently down my face. I didn't even realize I had been crying until I stopped talking. Capri is, too, based on her sniffling. She wraps her arms around my waist almost as if she's trying to piece me back together. She doesn't say anything, but then again what is there to say? Capri knows there is nothing she can say to fix any of it, so she just holds onto me which might be exactly what I need.

SEVENTEEN

Capri

In the middle of the night when I wake up, heat floods me. I attempt to kick my sheets off, but a heavy weight is on top of me making it impossible to move the sheets. The more awake I become, the more the events from last night return to me. Jayse's confession weighs heavily on my chest. My heart shatters for him because I can't even begin to imagine what he must have felt in those moments. The fear and grief of knowing your family is trapped and may not survive. It's horrible enough to think about the amount of grief he must carry around with him daily over the situation. I'm sure he can't escape his own mind, but to be as permanently scarred on the outside as you are on the inside...that's a heavy burden to carry.

Everything is starting to make sense now. The way everyone in town reacted to the two of us being seen with one another. I highly doubt that he's spent time in public with another person since the night of the fire. He believes the town blames him, but I have a feeling he's wrong. Blue Ridge views every resident as family. The night of the fire they lost two members, almost three. Something tells me that I'm sure they are glad he survived and, like me, they know he did everything he could to save Bradee and Sam.

We stayed in the cemetery for far too long. It was nearly one in the morning when we left. I led us out with Jayse following behind me the whole trip. We only stopped once and that was so Jayse could lock the gates of the cemetery back up. We didn't hit a single red light and there was no traffic. It was quiet and quick, but nerves wracked my body. I wasn't sure what to expect when we arrived at our homes. As I parked, so did Jayse. His motorcycle was directly behind my car. I gathered my belongings, but before I was finished Jayse was there, opening my door. Silence settled between us, but it wasn't awkward. It was more of a quiet understanding. I now understood him and why he was tortured and closed off from the world around him. I'm shocked that we have managed as much as we have.

One of his arms is tossed over my abdomen, his head resting on my shoulder. Right now, he seems at peace. There is no broody facial expression, no pinch of his eyes or fake smile on his lips. I hope that when he wakes, I find this same version because I understand him now. Slowly, I reach out and run one of my hands through his soft locks. He mumbles and snuggles deeper into me. The roughness of his growing beard scratches at my skin.

As I lie in bed staring at the ceiling, I can't help the feeling of contentment that washes over me. All of my life I've been running, searching for something to bring me that inner peace. Is it possible that Jayse is what I was searching for? Both of us have had difficult pasts, to say the least, but if we can overcome those together, then we might possibly have a chance at a future together. Thora jumps onto the bed. Jayse stirs some before popping open one eye. A lopsided smile appears on his face. "Hi, Bright Eyes."

I don't even try to fight the smile that pulls at my mouth. "Hey," I whisper into the dark.

Jayse leans up, resting on one elbow. His other hand runs through my hair. "I never thought this was possible."

My head turns so that I can press a light kiss into the palm of his hand. "That makes two of us. This feeling is odd for me, but it's what I've always been looking for."

His stormy gray eyes get sad. "I had it, but I never believed I'd find it again. I didn't think it was possible to get that lucky twice in my life. You're different. You always have been. From the moment I saw you when you were moving in here, I couldn't take my eyes off you."

I run a hand through his hair. "I believe that souls can find each other without our knowledge. Maybe, that's what this is. Our souls recognized each other before we truly did."

A small, thoughtful smile appears on his face, and he leans down and presses a kiss to my lips. I'm not sure if he means for it to become more but it does.

Hours later, I wake up to Thora snuggled under my chin and the rest of my bed empty and cold. A piece of paper was lying on my nightstand with Jayse's messy script running across it.

Capri: *I hated to leave but I had to get some work done. I'll see you soon, bright eyes.*

The smile on my face was contagious as I got up and ready for work.

My day at Bee's Batter was busy, but not insanely so. However, when I got off work Jayse's truck wasn't in his driveway so he must still be working. I considered texting him, but it seemed silly since I wasn't even sure what we were to one another right now. So instead, I headed up to my apartment. Thora happily greeted me as I headed upstairs to soak in a hot bubble bath for a bit. My feet were achy.

Just as I climbed out of the bathtub, I heard the doorbell ring out through the house. Quickly, I slipped on my oversized t-shirt and shorts and rushed downstairs. When I open the door, Jayse is standing there looking tired, but with a smile on his face and food in his hands. "I brought dinner."

"I see that. Come on in," I tell him, as I step away from the door. He puts the pizza, pasta and wing boxes on the table. "How was your day?"

Jayse sighs heavily. "Long, but okay. I finished up a couple of jobs, did an estimate on another one, and fixed my mom's car."

"Is her car okay?" I ask. I've seen Jayse's family a few times in the bakery. They're all very nice and welcoming. His mother reminds me of the kind of mother I always wanted.

He nods his head. "Yeah, it just needed new brakes and with dad's bad back, he has a hard time getting down there now."

I cross the room and without a second thought I wrap my arms around his waist and plant a kiss in the middle of his chest. "You're kind of awesome, do you know that?"

Jayse chuckles. "No, I didn't."

"Well, now you do." He wraps his arms around me and presses a kiss to the top of my head. His stomach growls in hunger loudly. I look up at him. "I think you need to eat."

"I'm afraid I'll forget to chew and just inhale it all," he admits. He seems a little embarrassed, but he shouldn't be. He's had a long day.

"That's okay too, just don't choke," I tease him with a laugh.

After we eat, Jayse heads across the alley to shower and change. He promises to be back later. While he's gone, I decide to finish the painting sitting on my easel. My hands itch from the absence of my creative outlet. I haven't been painting and normally that only makes me more anxious. Jayse has been a good distraction.

I take my seat in front of the easel and finish the painting. It's about to get the perfect new home.

EIGHTEEN

Jayse

As I walk into my house, I prepare for a wave of guilt. Surely, I'm not allowed to feel this content in life right now, even though it has been seven years since losing Bradee and Sam. However, as I enter, I still have a feeling of contentment settled within my soul. As I look over my shoulder, my eyes move to her window where she sits on the stool, paintbrush in hand, and coffee mug in the other. Thora sits on the window watching me. I never thought I would be allowed to even attempt to move on from my past life, but maybe it is possible after all. One last lingering look at the woman who has come in and completely changed my life before I head inside.

****

The next morning once I'm showered and dressed, I send a text to Capri wishing her a good day. I start to load my truck with the necessities for my job today and head out. My sister calls me on my way to the house. "Hey, Whit," I answer.

"Hello to you, too." The tone of her voice has me on high alert instantly. She's got that annoying sisterly sound like she knows something that I don't. I know that's not possible because there is nothing to know, but it still causes my body to tense up.

Silence fills the line just the sound of her TV in the background and my low playing music in the cab of my truck. Finally, I bite the bullet and ask, "What's going on?"

I can practically hear the smile in her voice. "Oh nothing, I just got off from work and I got the next two days off."

"Well, that's good and well earned. I'm glad you have some time to finally catch up on stuff and relax. You work too hard." Whitney always has. Even as kids, she worked extra hard to keep straight A's and be an outstanding citizen, always volunteering when she could. Whitney just always wanted to help the people around her, no matter what it ended up costing her in return.

She laughs. "I could say the same thing about you. You're always working and when you're not you're locked away in your house. It's not healthy."

"That's not entirely true." After I admit that to her, I regret it. There's a good chance that is exactly what she was wanting me to say.

Whitney scoffs. "It is, which is why I'm calling you. You need to come have lunch with me and mom today at the house. Dad has some kind of fishing trip planned with his friends so she's all alone and you know how she loves to cook."

It was true my mom did love to cook, and she was fantastic at it. Honestly, she could have opened a restaurant if she had wanted to, but she always said she never wanted that hassle. Instead, she would sign up for every bake sale or money raising food activity she could. "What time are we having this lunch?"

"Noon! I'm going to grab a quick nap before I head over there. We'll see you then." That tone is back in her voice, but I don't have time to question it before she disconnects the call.

Once I reach the house, I'm working on today I call Everett. "I'm actually heading in your direction. The wood you placed an order for came in, so I was going to drop it off for you."

"That's great news, but I'm actually not at home. I'm heading to a job. Do you want me just to swing by and grab it after I finish here?"

"No, I'll pop it in the shed. There's supposed to be a storm brewing today. I don't want it to get ruined before you even receive it." Everett hums along to the song on the radio.

I make a rash decision. "You know what, I'll see you in a few." I disconnect the call with Everett, then start to head back to my house as I ask my phone to dial Mrs.

Colson so I can let her know I'll be by after lunch. Luckily, she's very understanding as always. When I pull up to my house, Everett's truck is already there, but he's nowhere in sight which means, he already started moving the wood. I throw the truck in park and climb out. Jogging over to the bed of his truck I grab a couple of boards and head around back where I find Everett neatly stacking the wood in my work shed.

"I could have taken care of this Jayse. You didn't have to come back." Everett takes his baseball cap off his head and wipes the sweat with the back of his arm.

Placing the wood neatly in the stack I tell him, "I know, but it didn't sit right with me. Mrs. Colson was very understanding."

"I didn't know you were doing work for her."

My head bobs up and down. "I am. Her bathroom needed fixing really bad. I'm getting it taken care of."

Everett eyes me. "There's no way she can afford that kind of money."

"I didn't say I was charging her," I counter.

He chuckles while scratching at the stubble on his jaw. "You never fail to remind me that some of us never change."

"Shut up and help me move this wood." We work in silence for the next fifteen minutes until the wood is in the shed. "Do you want something to drink?"

"You got some water?" Everett asks.

I nod my head. The temperature isn't exactly warm, but we did work up a sweat moving the wood around.

"Yeah, come on inside and sit down for a few unless you need to be somewhere."

Everett glances at his watch. "No, I have a few hours before I have to do anything else." We head inside and I grab us bottles of water as we take a seat at the table. "So, do you want to talk about Capri?"

Everything in my body stops. The arm that was bringing the water to my mouth stops midair. My eyes flash to him and he's got a smirk on his face that I'd like to wipe right off him, but in all honesty if anyone is going to understand what I've been through, it's Everett. However, I can't just come out and discuss this so I'm going to play like I don't know what the hell he's talking about. "What do you mean?"

His eyebrows raise as he begins to laugh. "You only looked over towards her apartment about twenty times as we moved the wood around."

I shake my head and the denial comes to me instantly. "I did not."

"You did. Plus, you've been seen all over town with her. You might as well tell me what's going on." My mouth opens and closes multiple times before Everett speaks again. He must realize I'm at a loss for words. "I get it. Losing Diana killed me. Luckily, I got to keep Cayley, but you...you had to lose both in one sweep. The only life you'd ever known had suddenly vanished. I can't even imagine how you must have felt."

I sigh heavily. "For years, I've been trying to figure out what to do, who to be. I've been so lost. I honestly never thought I'd find someone I'd even want to try with again. In my mind it was always Bradee and I. We were the end game. She was all I had ever wanted until we had Sam. My life was perfect in my eyes when the fire happened..." My throat clogs and I look away.

"And everything changed. Not only were you injured, but you had lost everything that actually mattered." Everett has always been a great listener. He's great at filling in the blanks when I can't speak.

My head nods yes. "When I first started noticing Capri, right after she moved to Blue Ridge, I often felt so guilty. In my mind, I shouldn't be able to move on with how much I loved them. I fought it with everything I had. Then I started working on Bee's Batter and everything changed. Whatever had drawn me towards Capri to begin with was only growing stronger while I was around her. It got to the point where I couldn't deny it. Now, I've let her in."

"How far in?" he asks.

It's no secret about me and my time spent in the cemetery. "I took her there last night." I don't have to explain where "there" is. Everett just knows. His eyes widen. "She knows everything."

Silence settles between us as we stare at each other across the table. "I know it's hard, but it's also time. This will be good for you, and you deserve it. Let this happen. Don't try to run and don't try to push her away."

"I'm working on it and so is she but she has a past, too."

Everett nods his head. "Don't we all?"

After Everett leaves, I peek around the house before heading to my parents and Mrs. Colson. Everett's words hold a place in my head, running around in circles. I don't want to ruin this thing between Capri and I, but sometimes we can't stop our bad habits.

NINETEEN

Capri

My phone starts ringing, pulling me away from the painting. As I lay the paint brush back down, I realize how achy and stiff my body is, especially my fingers, from how long I've sat here working on this painting. It's always like that for me. I get lost in the colors and images in my mind that move on to the canvas. I can't even begin to count how many times I've lost most of my day in this same position. Forgetting to eat, drink, or even move.

I grab my phone off the windowsill and see it's Warbee. Thinking that she needs someone to work at the bakery I answer it. "Hey, Boss, what's up?"

"Nope, I'm not calling as your boss. I'm calling as your friend. You are coming with Teaganne and me," Warbee announces.

My eyebrows raise in suspicion. "To where?"

"That's a surprise," I hear Teaganne call from the background.

I sit down on the edge of the couch; nerves fill my body. "I'm not so good with surprises."

"I promise you'll love it. We are just going to have a girl's day so we can relax for a bit. We've all been running on empty between Teaganne and I's new company and then Bushels of Fun...there's been so much back-to-back. We've all earned a little down time to recharge and you're coming with us." I've worked with Warbee long enough to know that once she sets her mind on something there's not much chance of changing it unless you threaten Rocker. As much as I don't like surprises, I have to admit threatening Rocker seems a little extreme.

Sighing, I stand back up and begin to pace back and forth. "Okay, I guess I'm in."

"Yes, I knew you would be. Get dressed. We are like four minutes from your apartment. Meet us outside." The line goes dead, and I look down at my leggings and oversized t-shirt which is littered with holes. Not to mention, all of the paint from the years of art. I rush upstairs to put something else on. When I reach my closet, I realize the problem that I hadn't thought of until now is I don't know what to wear. I don't know where we're going or what we're doing. There could be a certain type of outfit I should wear, but surely if there was Warbee would have told me.

Finally, I just grab my favorite dark wash skinny jeans, cobalt blue long sleeve shirt, and a pair of black boots. I release my hair from the messy bun and try to fluff it out. I grab a longer necklace just because I feel like it needs something. It's a large eye with a blue crystal as the pupil. It's one of my favorites. I grab a pair of hoop earrings, my black leather jacket and scarf and head for the door, grabbing my purse off the table beside me as I head out.

The moment I step outside I spot Warbee and Teaganne. The shiny silver Lexus sedan is hard to miss and makes my Chevy Sonic look like a sore thumb. Teaganne comes from money, but she's also worked hard to get where she is now. She's earned her Lexus, but I'd be lying if I said she didn't intimidate me because she does. Teaganne always seems so together. Most days I feel like a mess rolling around trying to figure out my life still.

I climb into the back seat and both, Warbee and Teaganne, turn around to greet me. "Are you ready to relax for a bit?" Teaganne asks. Her long, raven colored hair is held back by a simple bronze colored headband. She looks stunning with barely any makeup. Teaganne has always been friendly and welcoming, but Warbee and Teaganne have been best friends for so long, I can't help feeling like a third wheel sometimes.

"What exactly are we doing?" I ask.

Warbee laughs. "Okay, I'll tell you and ruin the surprise. Teaganne and I took on a job. Teaganne has been helping decorate the new business and BeeTeag is going to help launch it when it opens in a few weeks. So, Lillie Maymers, offered us a trial run at it. She's giving a select few the option to come try it out first. Kind of like a trial run to figure out any issues she might have before she opens officially."

My mind wanders what Lillie is opening. There are a number of things that could be happening. I knew there was a building she was looking at in town. We discussed its location with the relaxing view of the mountains one time at the bakery. The building was older and needed a lot of work which was something she wasn't sure she wanted to take on. "Okay, that's great, but what is it?"

Teaganne laughs. "You really don't like surprises, do you?" She glances at me in her rearview mirror. Her honey-colored eyes meet mine. I'm not sure what she sees but she decides to tell me. "It's a day spa."

"A spa? Really?"

Warbee bobs her head excitedly. "I can't wait. I'm so excited."

It's moments like these that really put a damper on my mood. I feel so out of the loop. My life experiences have been so little compared to most people in my life. Normally, it doesn't bother me but then something as simple as a spa day happens and I'm reminded of how much I've missed out on because I'm always working, trying to make ends meet or running from my past and bad decisions. I've never been to a spa, but I'm afraid to admit that. I'm sure they both could call a spa their second home. I give a short laugh and a quiet comment, "I can tell," from my place in the backseat.

We pull up to the older building that has definitely had a face lift. The two-story white brick looks refreshing. Teaganne parks in VIP parking and we climb out and head inside. The calming scents of lavender and mint fill my senses as we enter. The room is large, open, and inviting and decorated in a white, baby blue and mint green theme. It's a very calming atmosphere. Lillie, a leggy, strawberry blonde, blue eyed, ex-beauty queen comes around the corner and greets us. "I'm so happy y'all could make it. Please, remember this is a trial run for us. If you have any issues or suggestions, please let me know. Let me officially welcome you to Skyscape Spa."

Teaganne works out our schedules with Lillie. Warbee joins me as we sip on cucumber, lemon and mint infused water. It tastes amazing. Warbee leans in. "I'm so excited. I've never been to a spa before!"

I'm pretty sure my jaw hits the floor at that confession. In the car I assumed a spa would be second nature for Warbee. "What do you mean?"

Warbee looks at me and laughs. "I've never been to a spa before." She bumps my shoulder with hers. "See, you aren't the only one."

"You knew?" I ask. A blush of embarrassment floods my cheeks.

She gives me a small smile. "I could tell by your reaction in the car. Things like this are so common for Teaganne, but not for me. Baking was always my escape from reality, my relaxation place. Teaganne loves the spa so when we got invited, we knew we had to come and try it out. Plus, Lillie really wants this to work, and she totally deserves for it to work, so if we can help her out, we should."

"You know, you're one of the main reasons I stayed in Blue Ridge." The statement just falls out of my mouth. I hadn't meant to tell her. Mostly, because I worried it would seem odd, but it's out of the bag now.

Warbee looks at me. "Really?"

"Yeah, I mean, Blue Ridge is great and I felt at home and safe here for the first time in my life, but it was you that made me want to stay. You were so kind and understanding, even though you didn't have my back story. You welcomed me without any questions and just made me feel like part of the family. I'd never had that before."

When I look over, Warbee's eyes are shining with unshed tears. "Those are the kindest words. Thank you, Capri. Honestly, I always try to be the person I would want if I was lost or alone in this world. A simple act of kindness can go a long way, but this world has lost a lot of the kindness it once had and it's disappointing. I'm so glad you stayed."

"Me, too." She links her arm with mine and we grab a glass of water for Teaganne and head in her direction.

Warbee leans in. "I think, though, some of the reason you stayed was out of your hands." I give her a questioning look. "Jayse. I think the universe knew Jayse needed you and in return you needed him. I'm glad that it seems the two of you have finally found each other. I'm so happy for both of you. Just know I'm always in your corner."

At the mention of Jayse, butterflies appear in my stomach. I won't deny what she says because it feels like she just might be right. I may never agree out loud because that feeling of vulnerability is not something I'm good with, but I do think Jayse and I needed each other and I'm excited to see where it takes us.

TWENTY

Jayse

After I finish up with Everett, I head over to my parents' house. When I pull up to the one story, white and black house I notice Whitney's car is already in the driveway. As I climb out of my truck, the smell of BBQ fills the air. I take a deep breath and breathe it in. My stomach instantly growls with hunger. For whatever reason, I grab my cell phone and send a quick text to Capri to tell her I'm having lunch with my family, and I hope she's having a good day.

As I head towards the front door, my phone alerts me of an incoming text message. When I open it, I see she's having a spa day with Warbee and Teaganne. There is a picture attached of the three of them, all in fluffy white robes. I chuckle and save the picture to my phone. "Well, someone certainly has my baby boy smiling." My mom's voice seems to come out of thin air. I didn't even realize she was waiting for me behind the screen door. I look up and she smiles.

"Hi, Mama." She opens the door for me and pulls me into her arms. She's a tiny lady with a gray pixie cut and big gray eyes. "How are you?"

She gives me a huge smile, the one that causes the wrinkles around her eyes to appear. "I'm better now that we're all here together. Come on in."

The house I grew up in is modest in comparison to a lot of the homes in Blue Ridge. Lots of money floats around this small mountain town. My childhood home is a three bedroom, two bath, fourteen hundred square foot place of bliss for me. It's always been my safe haven. A few years ago, my dad, Everett, and I completely redid the inside and outside. It looks like a new, up-to-date house, but it still feels like home. My mom and I head through the house to the backyard. The deck-like porch is a summertime oasis, but in this case, we'll call it an autumn oasis. There's a slight chill in the air, but with the heat from the grill it seems just right. Whitney is sitting back, relaxing with a glass of sweet tea in hand. "Hey there, big brother," she calls out. My father looks over his shoulder at me. "There's my boy."

I smile, wave and greet them all. It's painfully obvious that I don't come around often enough. I always make sure to check on them and if they need me, I drop everything to be here, but I need to be better about actually coming by. Every time I do I feel guilty about their excitement of actually showing up. "Do y'all need help with anything else? Sorry, I'm a little late. Everett got my wood supply in, and we had to unload."

"How is Everett?" Whitney asks. A blush fills her cheeks, and she quickly adverts her eyes from me which leads me to wonder what that's all about. Everett spent years smitten with Whitney, but she never seemed interested. Now it seems that something might have changed with them. I know Everett said Whitney and he had been talking, but it definitely seems like they might have something going on.

After studying her for a few moments I reply, "He seems well. Just busy juggling the store and Cayley." Whitney nods her head but doesn't reply after that. "How's the fishing been, Dad?"

My dad looks over his shoulder and smiles at me. It's mischievous which must mean it's been good. "This time of the year seems to be the best time for me to fish. I catch more than what I need most days. Must be something in the air." My dad catches fish and then tosses them back in. For all he knows it might be the same fish he keeps catching, but I don't have the heart to tell him that. "The ribs are ready," he announces. I get up from my chair and head over to help him carry them to the table. One lonely hamburger bun sits on the plate.

"I see you still won't touch ribs," I tease Whitney.

She shrugs and scrunches up her nose. "It's weird."

"How is eating ribs any weirder than eating a hamburger?"

Whitney huffs. "I don't know, it just is. You shouldn't be so judgmental, Mister."

My head falls back in laughter. "Okay, I'll keep that in mind." I place a rack of ribs on each plate before placing Whitney's hamburger on the last. As I hand it to her, I tell her, "Here is you're not so weird hamburger."

She takes the plate while mumbling "shut up" at me. I laugh and take a seat next to my mom. She pats my hand. She still smells of lilac and her skin is just as soft as ever. She's always just how I remember. "So, are you going to tell us about the girl?"

Choking on the sip of sweet tea I had just taken; I work to clear my throat. My mom pats me on the back until it clears up. "What?" I ask.

"The girl...Capri is her name, right?" My mother eyes me expectantly.

I'm just about to pretend I don't know what she's talking about when Dad chimes in. "Don't even bother denying it. I ran into Isaac, and he told me about your midnight outing with her. It seems like this could become something serious if you're taking her to the cemetery so we felt like we should know about her."

So, this is why Whitney had asked me to come here for lunch. Whitney gives me an apologetic smile. I sigh. "Yes, her name is Capri. Yes, I'm sure it could get serious, but that doesn't mean it will."

"Why not?" my mother asks. "Don't you like her?"

Images of Capri flash through my mind like a slideshow. "Yes, very much so."

"Then what's the problem?" she asks again.

I meet all three of their eyes. I know they mean well, but right now I really want to leave. I'm not ready for these types of conversations. "Y'all know what the problem is. Why did you go to all the trouble of fixing lunch if it was basically an intervention?"

"Son, it's not an intervention unless you're on drugs, which we can discuss that, too," my dad says, as he wipes barbeque sauce from his mouth.

Shaking my head, I stand up abruptly. Anxiety, guilt, and grief mix within my body causing my legs to itch with the need to run. My mom stands up next to me. Her hand wrapping around my scarred elbow. "Please, let it go. You're closing off again. I miss that smile I saw when you were coming up to the door. That was my boy."

I start to shake my head again. The denial is always on the tip of my tongue in these moments, but Whitney stops me. "You took Capri to the cemetery and told her about Bradee and Sam, right?" I nod my head. "You've been spending time with her on a regular basis, right?" Again, I nod my head. "You care about her more than you are willing to admit right now, right?" I don't move. I just stand there staring down at my plate of untouched food. "You're moving on like you're supposed to. You're doing exactly what Bradee would have wanted and it's the same thing you would have wanted for her if it had been you that died in that fire, and she had survived. There is absolutely nothing wrong with what you're feeling."

"Bradee was supposed to be my forever. I can't just forget her," I say quietly. I hate how sad and broken my voice sounds right now, but it feels as if there is a knife twisting around in my gut.

My dad clears his throat. "You will never forget her. None of us will. She was a part of this family and loved by every one of us. They both were but keeping yourself isolated from everyone is not doing her memory justice. Bradee loved life and she lived it to the fullest. She didn't hide away from the world. Make her proud, Jayse. Be the man she fell in love with to begin with."

Those words make me take a moment and think. He's right, as hard as that is to admit, he is. I loved Bradee and Sam with every fiber of my being, but how I have been living is the last thing she'd want for me. We talked about it throughout the years, what we would want the other to do if something happened to us. We were both adamant about moving on and living life and finding love again. At the time, I just agreed to her terms because I couldn't picture my life with anyone but her, but now Capri is a game changer.

Slowly, I sink back down into my seat. I eat lunch with my family before heading to work on Mrs. Colson's house. I work until the sun goes down and the stars come out. My mind and body are occupied with two completely different things. By the time I get into my truck, my body is exhausted, but my mind is wide awake with excitement of seeing Capri. I checked my phone, but I don't have anything missed from her. I stopped to grab some sweets from the bakery, but she's not working so I'll surprise her when I get home.

My dad's words still play in my mind and for the first time in what feels like forever...I'm content and at peace.

TWENTY-ONE

Capri

The spa was amazing and relaxing. I learned so much about Teaganne and I have to admit that once the day was done, I found I didn't really feel like much of a third wheel anymore. We joked about being Charlie's Angels, took some selfies to help advertise the spa on social media, and relaxed, which was something I hadn't truly done in a very long time. As we get situated in Teaganne's car Warbee announces, "I'm hungry!"

Teaganne and I burst out laughing because Warbee literally sounds like Teaganne's little girl, Seraphina. It's the same thing she says every time she steps into Bee's Batter. "Well, I guess you know where Seraphina gets it from," I tease Teaganne from the backseat.

"Apparently. Okay, I guess I'll feed you," she teases. We head into town and decide Burger Hop sounds good until we pull up and the place is packed!

"Oh goodness! I'm going to starve if we have to wait this long." Warbee must really be hungry.

Teaganne sighs and scans the area. "There aren't a lot of choices right now. A lot of them are closed because of the weekend, and then everything else is full because the Sip and Smack is closed due to the gas leak. We can go to Blue Bar. Are you okay with bar food?"

Warbee moves her glasses down her nose to look at her best friend. Warbee's look says, 'really?' "It's food, right?"

"Technically, that's up for debate, but yes it resembles food." Warbee looks back at me and laughs at my comment.

"Okay, Capri isn't wrong, but yes let's go there." Warbee turns up the radio as we head towards Blue Bar. We sing along. As we pull up, I'm sure Warbee is happy to see that the bar isn't as full as Burger Hop. Now my stomach has begun to grumble in hunger.

We climbed out and head inside. Blue Bar is no different than any other bar you could go into. Country music blasts through the speakers, filling the area, along with the stench of stale smoke and beer. The sound of pool being played on the tables and darts mix with the country music along with the chatter and laughter of the customers. Timber, one of the local guys and bartender, greets us from behind the counter. "Sit wherever you like, ladies, I'll be there in a minute to grab y'alls order."

We take a seat and Timber comes around a couple minutes later. We order just about everything on the menu and sodas. After he leaves the table, we sit back. Teaganne eyes Warbee. "Okay, what's going on with you?"

"What do you mean?" Warbee asks, but her tone is too defensive, giving away that there is in fact something going on.

I tilt my head as I wonder what it could be. "What is going on?"

Warbee sighs. "Okay, so Rocker and I are adopting a baby."

"What?" Teaganne and I squeal in unison. Warbee and Rocker will never be able to have children of their own naturally due to Warbee's medical past, so this is huge and I'm sure something she's overjoyed about, yet she looks terrified right now. "What's wrong?" I ask.

Her eyes meet mine. "I'm just worried that something is going to go wrong, and it won't work out."

Teaganne reaches across the table and lays her hand over Warbee's while giving it a little squeeze. "It'll work out because the two of you deserve it. I'm so happy for you."

I reach over and lay my hand on top of theirs. "I am, too. I can't think of two people who will be better parents."

"You mean, aside from Keefer and I," Teaganne says, with a teasing tone.

Warbee, Teaganne, and I laugh. "Yes, of course, besides y'all."

"How's everything going since y'all moved in with Keefer officially? How did Silas and Seraphina adjust?" Warbee asks.

Teaganne smiles and there isn't a trace of sadness or stress behind it. When she first arrived back in Blue Ridge from New York City, her smiles always seemed a little forced, but now they seem sincere, and she seems content. "Great, actually. I think they've viewed Keefer like a father for a while now, so it feels natural for them. We have a good dynamic going. He's officially adopting them in a couple of months. The paperwork is already sitting on my lawyer's desk."

Warbee squeals. "That's amazing."

"It really is. I'm happy for you, too," I tell Teaganne.

Teaganne smiles and takes a deep breath. "It's such a change. I'm so completely happy with my decision to come back home. So now the question is about you and Jayse?"

My shoulders lift in a shrug as Timber comes over with two trays of food and drinks. After he arranges everything on the table between us, we fix our plates and I answer. "I don't know. I didn't intend for anything to happen between us. Years ago, I made myself a promise that I wouldn't try the relationship thing again, but it's looking like I might be breaking that promise."

"Sometimes we make promises in the moment that are right at that point in time, but they aren't meant to be there forever."

"I'm guessing he told you about his past," Teaganne comments.

I nod my head. "Yes, about Bradee, Sam, and the fire. I can't even imagine how that must have felt. Getting the backstory definitely helped me make sense and understand him better."

"I'm glad you two found each other," Warbee comments.

"Me, too."

As we finish eating, the sounds of sirens flood into the bar with us, drowning out the music. Everyone falls silent. Cooper, one of the local cops jumps up and rushes to the door. Timber hollers, "What happened?"

"Fire at Clark's building." Cooper's eyes swing to mine. "Capri, don't you live there?"

Everything in my body freezes. The only thing I can manage to do is nod. I hear the commotion around me as Teaganne rushes to pay Timber and Warbee pulls me from my chair and ushers me to Teaganne's car. I can't make sense of anything as the tears painfully clog my throat. The smoke flows into the night sky. I feel like it's clogging my very own lungs even though I'm nowhere near it. Everything I own is in that apartment. Thora is in that apartment. My heart pounds erratically.

As we pull up, there are so many onlookers, fire trucks, and police cars that we have to park blocks away. We jog towards the alley where even more commotion is taking place. I rush towards Cooper. "My cat is in the apartment."

He nods. "I'll notify them. Do you know if Ella Mae was home?"

I shake my head. "I haven't been here all day, but her car isn't here."

My eyes roam as the firefighters rush inside. I can hear them yelling. "He just ran in there. He grabbed my mask and took off. I didn't even have time to try and stop him."

Confusion and panic as the sinking feeling of who they could be talking about takes over. Warbee and Teaganne have caught up to me. Both of them rub soothing circles on my back. I continue to scan the area and that's when I notice Whitney and Everett standing off to the side watching the flames dance against the night sky. Whitney is sobbing. I rush forward. "Where's Jayse?"

Everett's eyes go wide. Whitney stutters unable to say anything. "He's inside. He went after you."

"What? Why?" I scream.

"Your car was here; your phone was off. He thought you were trapped," Everett says.

My phone had died while at the spa. I spin around and take off as fast as I can towards the building. Screaming his name over and over. A pair of strong arms wrapped around my waist to hold me back. They're wrong. They're not his arms. The skin is too smooth as I try to push him away. I scream Jayse's name until my voice goes hoarse and finally, I collapse onto the ground. Cooper, the one who stopped me, goes to the ground with me. Broody, tortured, afraid of fire Jayse ran into the burning building because of me, for me. In this moment, I know my heart found its home, but I don't know if it'll still be there when the flames die out.

TWENTY-TWO

Jayse

Brightness tries to break through my sleep, the light trying to break through my eyelids. My head pounds, body aches from something I can't remember. Taking a deep breath, my chest feels tight and I begin to cough. The smell of antiseptic and cleaner fills my nose. Definitely not my house. No, this place smells like a medical facility. Something heavy and warm is on my right hand. I lift my eyelid slightly and peek through. Capri.

Everything floods back at one time.

Arriving home to the smell of smoke. Everett pulling in behind me after hearing a fire being called in on the scanner for Clark's building. My heart stopping completely because it felt like the whole world had stopped spinning on its axis. As I rushed around my house with Everett on my heels, the flames were on the bottom floor of Capri's building. Whitney jogged down the alley. I heard her say something about being on her way home and heard about the fire, so she came in case they needed help.

I scan the area and easily notice Capri's car sitting in its parking space. I'm just about to dart across the alley, when Everett grabs my arm, yanking me back. I spin around to face him, my hands balled into fists. Just as I'm about to let them fly, the ear-piercing sounds of fire truck sirens fill the quiet night. That sound used to be second nature to me, but right now it feels completely foreign. I watch as the fire truck parks and my previous co-workers begin to file out, dressed in gear and rushing to handle their given tasks. Something twists in my gut. A familiarity, a yearning to be part of that formation once more. Some part of me knows they are moving as fast as they can, but it feels like they move in slow motion.

Everett and Whitney's heads are close together, obviously discussing something. My heart feels like it's trapped inside that building. My eyes roam once more trying to find Capri, but I don't spot her anywhere. Without another thought I grab a discarded mask and rush forward. I hear people hollering for me, but I just move faster. I'm breaking every safety protocol I've ever been taught, but it doesn't matter. I can't let what happened to Bradee and Sam happen to Capri. I just can't.

The heat from the fire hits me immediately. My skin burns and aches, sweat covers every part of my body within a moment's time. I rush forward carefully to avoid the biggest of flames. I take the stairs two at a time as I head up to Capri's apartment. It's smoky on the second floor but the flames haven't reached this high yet. Her front door is locked so I stand back and kick at it until it starts to give. Finally, the

171

wood cracks. Movement from downstairs is heard but I don't know if the building is caving to the fire's anger or if it's the firefighters, I used to call brothers. Once I'm inside, I pull the mask off my face. The smoke chokes me instantly. If Capri is up here, there's a good chance she's unconscious from smoke inhalation. Inside my chest my heart slams around erratically. Something orange darts across the floor towards me. Thora. I scoop her into my arms and move further into the apartment. There's no sign of Capri. The heat has become more predominant which means the fire is closer to the top floor now. In Capri's art corner I see a picture. The colors draw me closer because they mimic that of a fire. In the middle is a faceless man, shirtless, and scarred with huge bird wings coming out from behind him. Longer hair dances around the missing face. It's a Phoenix rising from the flames of the fire. It's me as a Phoenix. That's how she sees me. This woman has my heart, but I may never get the chance to tell her. She's clearly not here so I rush back towards the front door with Thora in my arms, but the stairwell is consumed by the flames as they dance the deadly dance, as they make their way up the stairs. Quickly, I move back towards the window. The heat is insane. My lungs and eyes burn, but I dropped the mask somewhere and I have no clue where it is.

I drop to my knees and crawl towards the window. I'm almost there when I see a ladder appear. Thora is barely moving in my arms, but I still cling to her. My body is growing heavy with exhaustion and lack of oxygen. My mind swims until I can't take it anymore. I collapse on the floor. Apologizing to Capri and Thora.

As I open my eyes, I take in the room around me. I'm definitely in the hospital. Capri is here so she's alive. My body sags in relief. Slowly, my free hand moves to stroke the silky strands of her hair. Capri stirs and her large seafoam green eyes look up at me. Moisture instantly builds, cascading down her cheeks. "Jayse," she says, in a hoarse whisper.

"Hey there, Bright Eyes." My voice is as hoarse as hers. I give her a smile and she stands up, launching herself into my arms. Her arms wrap around my neck as the sobs wrack her body. I pull her closer, never wanting to let her go again.

"I thought we lost you. When they pulled you out of the window you weren't moving." Her voice hiccups and I hate myself for scaring her so badly.

I pull her back and cup her face with my hands. "I'm here. I'm okay."

"Why'd you run in there? You could have gotten killed."

My answer is simple. "I thought you were in there, Capri. Your car was there so I just went. I didn't even think about it." That's the truth. "How's Thora?"

Carpi laughs. "She's okay. She's with your parents. You saved her."

"You saved me," I counter.

She shakes her head. "We saved each other."

Maybe, she's right. I'll always say she saved me, but maybe this beautiful woman needed a little saving, too. I'm more than glad to be the one to do that for her.

Something else happened though. When I rushed into those crackling flames, I found the part of myself I thought I had lost. In one night, I thought I had lost everything and at that time I had, but I've rebuilt something now and this version of me has finally found himself again, in large part because of the angel with the bright eyes I'm currently holding in my arms.

EPILOGUE

Capri

As I wake up freezing, I curl into Jayse. I swear, he's like my own personal space heater. I love it. Autumn has given way to winter, and the first snow has hit the ground. It was coming down heavily last night as we climbed into bed. We haven't had time to get the heat fixed in the house since we've only been here a couple of weeks. After Jayse was released from the hospital, it became obvious I didn't have much to go back home to. I had Thora and my car, most of everything inside my apartment had been severely smoke damaged, but that was okay. Jayse and Thora had survived and that's all that matters. Although, I hated that Jayse never got to see his picture.

We loaded up into his truck and I drove him to his house. He had looked over at me with those stormy gray eyes. "I think you should move in with me."

I remember not breathing and my mouth going instantly dry. "What?"

"You don't have a place now. Stay with me and we'll start looking for a place together." Jayse made it sound so easy. A part of me was hesitant, but the larger part of me knew that I didn't want to spend any more time away from him than necessary now. I was no longer concerned about breaking the promise to myself. Warbee had been right. I needed it at the time when I made it, but I didn't need it now. I took a deep breath and looked over at Jayse.

"Okay, sounds like a plan."

That's exactly what we did. We found a place pretty quickly. An older home with all the classic charm I love but it did need some fixing up. Thankfully, Jayse was perfect for that. However, getting around to all the stuff had been a challenge between the bakery, Warbee and Rocker's wedding, Teaganne and Keefer's engagement, holidays, and getting settled into our place. I also can't forget to mention that I'm preparing for my first art showing in Atlanta later this month, and that Jayse is officially a firefighter again. He is still the town's handyman, but only when he's not at the station. Things have been a whirlwind, but every time I get to take a minute and watch Jayse, I do. Coming so close to losing him was overwhelming and eye opening. Capri Owens will run no more.

I really need to pull myself out of this warm bed and move towards the art room that Jayse was working on for me yesterday. Teaganne and Warbee hired me right after the fire to do a couple of custom pieces for Lillie, the owner of Skyscape Spa. Well, it turned out that one of her clients owns a pretty popular art museum in Atlanta and she loved my pieces. Next thing I knew I had a show scheduled and an actual deadline. Then Warbee and Teaganne signed me onto their event and design planning business as their top artist for painted art pieces. My life here has come full circle I feel like.

Luckily, Jayse's family welcomed me with open arms. I can only imagine what they were thinking. For years, I had been the odd girl out in Blue Ridge with my crazy colored hair and band t-shirts. I was a loner and didn't get out much except to work. I'm sure they were hesitant about Jayse and I, but they never once said anything. They let it play out as it needed to. After Jayse got released from the hospital, we went to his childhood home and picked up Thora. It was then that I actually felt like I belonged in this little family. Whitney had become one of my best friends. Warbee, Teaganne, Whitney and I all do a girls movie night once a week (when schedules and kids allow it). That's probably going to change with Warbee and Rocker getting their baby soon.

I smile to myself as I take a deep breath. Carefully, I slip out of the bed, bundle up the best I can in the ice-cold house and make my way to the art room. The room sits on the back half giving me the picture-perfect view of mountains as well as every sunrise and sunset. The windows cover the majority of the room. As I open the door, I take a deep breath because this is one of my dreams. When I open the door, a slight scream escapes me before I pull it back in. Sitting there on the easel in the middle of the room is my picture of Jayse, my Phoenix.

"I'm sure it's still smoke damaged, but I couldn't let them toss it." Jayse's voice comes from behind me.

I turn around. "Were you awake the whole time?"

He shakes his head. His long hair is gone now. "No, I woke up as you left the bed then realized where you were heading. I wanted to witness your reaction."

"How did you get it?" I ask. Letting go of that painting was one of the hardest things I had ever done. I had wanted Jayse to see it so badly.

"Liam, one of my old buddies from the station, got it for me. That picture made me realize so much that night. It helped get me out of your apartment. I couldn't let go."

I don't even fight the smile that pulls on my mouth. "I wanted you to see it so badly. I didn't know you saw it."

Jayse nods his head. "I saw it. It's actually the last thing I saw before everything went black."

I walk into his arms, and they wrap around me like a warm blanket. My protection, that odd sense washing over me. Jayse holds me like I'm treasured, as if I'm valuable and that's something I've never had before. He protects me with every fiber of his being. Jayse is one of the good ones. He's one of the ones I had been searching for. I pull back and look at him. "I love you." Those three words roll off my tongue so easily because it's right. There are no expectations on my love for him. It's unconditional and it's real.

Jayse smiles. "I love you, Bright Eyes." His lips find mine in the middle of the room. A dream come true; the main one I was always running from place to place trying to find.

Blue Ridge wasn't my destination. It was meant to be a stop on the journey, but it snuck into my heart slowly and quietly. The people became important and made me feel like I mattered. Traditions the town held made me feel like I was a part of the community. Blue Ridge was the place I never knew I needed, and it held the one thing I was always looking for...love. Love for myself, for someone else, and for a place that makes you feel like you belong.

Acknowledgements

First of all, thank you to Kingston Publishing for their continued belief in my books. All of their hard work is why you are currently holding this book (in whatever format). I couldn't do this without them.

To my mom and mema, thank you so much for always believing in me. Y'all always made me believe I could achieve whatever goal I had and because of that…. I did!

To my beta readers…Mom, Pat and Mary…thank you for always hanging in there while I make small and big changes. I run around with new ideas and constantly change at least one of my characters' names at least twice. They sit back and let me without ever complaining.

To my two guardian angels, Auntie and Vannalynn, thank you for always watching out for me. I know the two of you are probably making heaven a whole lot more fun, but we miss you here.

To my readers…y'all rock! I most definitely couldn't do this without you. It's your support. It's your questions about certain characters that keeps me going!

Thank you to everyone involved!!

About the Author

Stephanie Nichole lives in a small town with her family in New Mexico. She graduated college in 2010 with a degree in business and accounting. However, her true passion is all things book related. As a student English and Literature were her favorite subjects. Weekly library trips with her mother also helped instill her love for books. Stephanie would look forward to summer most of all, not because she was out of school but for the summer reading groups at her local library.

After a friend's encouragement she started her author journey in 2016.

Stephanie is an avid book, music and old Hollywood movie lover. When she's not busy reading or writing she's probably binge watching Netflix or PassionFlix. Some of her favorite authors are Edgar Allan Poe, Abbi Glines, Colleen Hoover, Alessandra Torre, Nicholas Sparks and F. Scott Fitzgerald.

Stephanie also loves to connect with her readers on social media.

Reader's group: https://bit.ly/StephanieNicholeRG
Newletter: https://bit.ly/StephanieNicholeNL
Author page: https://bit.ly/StephanieNicholeFB
Bookbub: https://bit.ly/StephanieNicholeBB
Amazon: https://amzn.to/2WF23P0
Instagram: https://bit.ly/StephanieNicholeIG
Twitter: https://bit.ly/3dToJ4l
Goodreads: https://bit.ly/StephanieNicholeGR

Also by the Author

The James Brothers Series:
Pedal to the Metal
Breaking the Limits
Force of Impact
Need for Speed
Finish Line

The Furiously Fast Series:
Full Throttled

The Dark Prophecy Series:
Magicals
Captured
Ignite

Bloody Mary's Curse:
Becoming Bloody Mary
Breaking Bloody Mary

The Blue Ridge Series
Autumn Skies and Pumpkin Pies
Autumn Wishes and Pumpkin Kisses
Autumn Leaves and Pumpkins Please

Other Titles:
Hell on the Highway
Thin Ice

Stephanie Nichole

True Lies
Chord Changes
Lost and Found
Red
Underland
Redeeming Air
Witch House

About the Publisher

Kingston Publishing Company, founded by C.K. Green and Michelle Areaux, is dedicated to providing authors an affordable way to turn their dream into a reality. We publish over 100+ titles annually in multiple formats including print and ebook across all major platforms.

We offer every service you will ever need to take an idea and publish a story. We are here to help authors make it in the industry. We want to provide a positive experience that will keep you coming back to us. Whether you want a traditional publisher who offers all the amenities a publishing company should or an author who prefers to self-publish, but needs additional help – we are here for you.

Now Accepting Manuscripts!
Please send query letter and manuscript to:
submissions@kingstonpublishing.com

Visit our website at www.kingstonpublishing.com